MARK

Getting to Know *Jesus*

A Guided Discovery for Groups and Individuals

Kevin Perrotta

LOYOLAPRESS.

CHICAGO

LOYOLAPRESS.

3441 N. ASHLAND AVENUE
CHICAGO, ILLINOIS 60657

Nihil Obstat
Reverend John G. Lodge, S.S.L., S.T.D.
Censor Deputatus
April 10, 2000

Imprimatur
Most Reverend Raymond E. Goedert, M.A., S.T.L., J.C.L.
Vicar General
Archdiocese of Chicago
April 10, 2000

The *Nihil Obstat* and *Imprimatur* are official declarations that a book is free of doctrinal and moral error. No implication is contained therein that those who have granted the *Nihil Obstat* and *Imprimatur* agree with the content, opinions, or statements expressed.

The Scripture quotations contained herein are from the New Revised Standard Version Bible: Catholic Edition, copyright © 1993 and 1989 by the Division of Christian Education of the National Council of the Churches of Christ in the U.S.A. Used by permission. All rights reserved. Subheadings in Scripture quotations have been added by the author.

The Greek text of John Chrysostom's sermon on the transfiguration (p. 47) can be found in *Patrologia Graeca*, vol. 58, edited by J.-P. Migne. Translation by the author.

The Latin text of Bede's commentary on Mark (p. 59) can be found in *Corpus Christianorum Series Latina*, vol. 120 (Turnhout, Belgium: Typographi Brepols, 1960). Translation by the author.

The Latin text (with an English translation) of Thomas More, *Concerning the Sorrow, Weariness, Fear, and Prayer of Christ before His Arrest* (p. 60) can be found in Clarence H. Miller, trans., *The Complete Works of St. Thomas More*, vol. 14, pt. 1 (New Haven, Conn.: Yale University Press, 1976). Translation by the author.

Interior design by Kay Hartmann/Communique Design
Illustration by Charise Mericle

ISBN 0-8294-1447-9

Printed in the United States of America

00 01 02 03 04 / 10 9 8 7 6 5 4 3 2 1

Contents

How to Use This Guide

You might compare this booklet to a short visit to a national park. The park is so large that you could spend months, even years, getting to know it. But a brief visit, if carefully planned, can be enjoyable and worthwhile. In a few hours you can drive through the park and pull over at a handful of sites. At each stop you can get out of the car, take a short trail through the woods, listen to the wind blowing in the trees, get a feel for the place.

In this booklet we'll drive through the Gospel of Mark, making half a dozen stops along the way. At those points we'll proceed on foot, taking a leisurely walk through the selected passages. The readings have been chosen to take us to the heart of Mark's message about Jesus.

After each discussion we'll get back in the car and take the highway to the next stop. "Between Discussions" pages summarize the portions of Mark that we will pass along the way.

This guide provides everything you need to explore Mark in six discussions—or to do a six-part exploration on your own. The introduction on page 6 will prepare you to get the most out of your reading. The weekly sections feature key passages from Mark, with explanations that highlight what his words mean for us today. Equally important, each section supplies questions that will launch you into fruitful discussion, helping you both to explore Mark for yourself and to learn from one another. If you're using the booklet by yourself, the questions will spur your personal reflection.

Each discussion is meant to be a *guided discovery.*

Guided. None of us is equipped to read the Bible without help. We read the Bible *for* ourselves but not *by* ourselves. Scripture was written to be understood and applied in and with the Church. So each week "A Guide to the Reading," drawing on the work of both modern biblical scholars and Christian writers of the past, supplies background and explanations. The guide will help you grasp Mark's message. Think of it as a friendly park ranger who points out noteworthy details and explains what you're looking at so you can appreciate things for yourself.

Discovery. The purpose is for *you* to interact with Mark's Gospel. "Questions for Careful Reading" is a tool to help you dig into the Gospel and examine it carefully. "Questions for Application" will help you consider what Mark means for your life here and now. Each week concludes with an "Approach to Prayer" section that helps you respond to God's Word. Supplementary "Living Tradition" and "Saints in the Making" sections offer the thoughts and experiences of Christians past and present in order to show you what the Gospel has meant to others—so that you can consider what it might mean for you.

How long are the discussion sessions? We've assumed you will have about an hour and a half when you get together. If you have less time, you'll find that most of the elements can be shortened somewhat.

Is homework necessary? You will get the most out of the discussions if you read the weekly material in advance of each meeting. But if participants are not able to prepare, have someone read the "What's Happened" and "Guide to the Reading" sections aloud to the group at the points where they occur in the weekly material.

What about leadership? If you happen to have a world-class biblical scholar in your group, by all means ask him or her to lead the discussions. But in the absence of any professional Scripture scholars, or even accomplished biblical amateurs, you can still have a first-class Bible discussion. Choose two or three people to be facilitators, and have everyone read "Suggestions for Bible Discussion Groups" before beginning (page 92).

Does everyone need a guide? a Bible? Everyone in the group will need their own copy of this booklet. It contains the sections of Mark that are discussed, so a Bible is not absolutely necessary—but each participant will find it useful to have one. You should have at least one Bible on hand for your discussion. (See page 96 for recommendations.)

How do we get started? Before you begin, take a look at the suggestions for Bible discussion groups (page 92) and individuals (page 95).

Unexpectedly Good News

Introducing Mark's Gospel

*O**ur Town,** Thornton Wilder's play about life in a New England village, opened on Broadway in 1938—well before most of us were buying theater tickets. But, growing up, each new generation of Americans has a fair chance of seeing or reading the play, because high school English teachers consider it a classic.

If *Our Town* was part of your school experience, you may recall that the stage manager appears at the beginning to set the scene. "The name of the town," he tells the audience, "is Grover's Corners, New Hampshire—just across the Massachusetts line: latitude 42°40'; longitude 70°37'. The first act shows a day in our town. The day is May 7, 1901. The time is just before dawn."

Later the manager brings a local professor on stage. He lectures the audience on the geology of the region and on the American Indians who lived there in centuries past.

Grover's Corners is a small place. But by providing it with real space-time coordinates and historical background, the playwright suggests that the lives of its residents have global significance.

Unlike Thornton Wilder, Mark did not put an informative stage manager at the beginning of his work. Mark dives into the action with hardly a preliminary. An introduction, however, might have helped orient us to the universal significance of his account. Apparently the other Gospel writers thought so. When, as scholars suppose, Matthew and Luke sat down to adapt Mark's Gospel, each added a couple of introductory chapters.

It is interesting to imagine what an *Our Town*–type opening to the Gospel of Mark would be like. I picture a guide standing on a hillside, looking down at a cluster of stone houses in the valley. "The name of this town," he says, "is Nazareth in Galilee. Galilee is a hilly region rising up from the Mediterranean to the west and descending eastward to the lake we call the Sea of Galilee. The lake's been there for five million years, since the earth split open and formed the Great Rift that stretches from Lebanon to Africa.

"This area's seen a lot of coming and going. Some thirty thousand years ago, Neanderthal people kept house in a cave yonder. It's almost two thousand years since Abraham traveled through these hills. Israelites settled here a thousand years ago. According to your modern reckoning, the year is A.D. 30."

If Mark had written a lead-in of this sort, it would have alerted us to the striking contrast between his story's small scale and its cosmic importance. In his Gospel, Mark reports events that seemed insignificant to most people at the time. He chronicles the brief notoriety and untimely death of a man from an obscure village—a man hardly mentioned in writings of the period outside the reports of his own followers. Yet before the Israelites appeared on the stage of history, before prehistoric people lived in caves, before the shaping of the earth, God had conceived the plan for humanity that reached its climax in this man, Jesus of Nazareth.

Like Thornton Wilder, Mark tells a story of universal significance, yet with a staggering difference. *Our Town* speaks to everyone because it explores our common human condition. The Gospel speaks to all of us because it tells about the measures the creator has taken to *alter* the human condition.

Pattern, promises, and expectations. Earlier I said that Mark did not give his Gospel an introduction. The reason may well be that he thought it already had one: the Scriptures of Israel. In his first verses, Mark indicates that the gospel, or "good news," of Jesus unfolded in accord with God's promises recorded in Israel's prophetic writings (1:2–3; biblical references are to Mark unless otherwise noted).

In Mark's view, Jesus brought what God had been doing with Israel to its climax. For this reason, getting some notion of God's dealings with Israel is indispensable if we are to understand who Jesus was and what he came to do. Let's look briefly, then, at the background.

The Scriptures of Israel, which Christians call the Old Testament, communicate a distinctive view of God and human beings. The Old Testament portrays a single creator, who has made humankind in his likeness, that is, designed to be in a relationship with him (Genesis 1:26). The Old Testament writings depict God as passionately committed to justice, yet forgiving; he is a God both majestic and merciful (Sirach 2:18). In the historical accounts and poetry of the Old Testament, we humans are portrayed as noble creatures who nevertheless have a sad tendency to set ourselves in conflict with God's purposes—and with each other.

The Old Testament shows that God focused his love for the human race on a small Near Eastern people called Israel. God rescued the Israelites from their enemies. He formed a covenant—a permanent, faithful bond—with them. He instructed them in how to worship and trust him and in how to live in faithfulness and peace with one another. The Israelites sometimes failed to respond wholeheartedly to God's initiatives. Periodically, the painful consequences of their sins afflicted the Israelites and impelled them to turn back to God. God then renewed his relationship with them and helped them in their need.

In 587 B.C. an accumulation of idolatries and social injustices among the people of Israel led to the destruction of Jerusalem by the Babylonians. This event was the watershed disaster in the history of Israel. God promised the Jews a splendid restoration. He would forgive their sins and even heal their sinful hearts (Jeremiah 31:31–34). Exiles would return to the land of Israel (Zephaniah 3:14–20). The Jerusalem temple would be rebuilt, and God would dwell there gloriously at the center of his people (Ezekiel 40–48). There would be prosperity for the people of Israel and defeat for their enemies (Zechariah 14). But God's blessings on the Jews would ripple out to the rest of the human race as well (Zechariah 8:20–23).

Six centuries later, at the beginning of the first century, these promises seemed to have been only half fulfilled. The land of Israel was part of the Roman Empire—a situation both oppressive and offensive to pious Jews. Yet, far from fading, the Jews' expectations for God's intervention intensified. Many looked for God to act on their behalf in a decisive, once-and-for-all transformation that would bring the history of humanity to a conclusion. God, they thought, would come to reign as king, inaugurating a final age of justice and peace. Even the dead would rise to enjoy new life. The expectations of God's action, combined with the Jews' painful political and economic circumstances, gave rise to numerous

insurrections against the Romans. Eventually two unsuccessful re-
bellions against Rome brought catastrophe on Jewish society in
the land of Israel (A.D. 66–70 and 132–135).

In this tense situation, around A.D. 30, Jesus made an
electrifying declaration: The period of waiting is over! God's reign
is about to arrive! (1:14–15). Jesus presented himself as the fulfillment of God's dealings with Israel. He acted as the fully authorized
representative of Israel's God. His proclamation of God's reign, his
miracles, his declarations of forgiveness, his gathering of disciples,
his teaching and symbolic actions—all should have signified to the
Jews of his time that their expectations for God's action on their
behalf were being fulfilled.

Expected, yet surprising. But it quickly became
apparent that Jesus was fulfilling Jewish expectations in a very
unexpected way. Jews of the time who observed Jesus and listened
to his preaching would have found several aspects of his "program"
surprising.

A messiah greater than expected. Jesus claimed to play
a larger role in the coming of God's kingdom than Jews had
expected any human being to play. Jews had various expectations
of how God would act on their behalf. Some thought God would
appoint a special leader, or messiah—perhaps more than one—
to spearhead his intervention. But Jews hardly expected a messiah
to act with the sweeping divine authorization that Jesus claimed to
have. God's healing, life-giving rule was becoming present in *Jesus'*
words and touch. The restoration of Israel began as men and
women took their places in the company of *Jesus'* disciples (see
3:33–35). Equally remarkable, Jesus gave authoritative rulings on
Israel's basic, God-given law (2:23–28). He forgave sins as God's
representative (2:1–11).

A more radical program. Surprisingly, Jesus did not aim at
a literal fulfillment of prophetic predictions of military triumph and
national sovereignty. Rather than raising an army to liberate the
land of Israel, Jesus promoted a kingdom without ties to any particular land. Jesus did bring liberation, but not from the Romans.

He liberated people from sicknesses, guilt, sinful attitudes, and broken relationships.

Nor did Jesus announce an intensification of God's presence in the temple in Jerusalem. In fact, he performed an action in the temple symbolizing that its usefulness was at an end (11:15–17).

Jesus bypassed the Mosaic rule permitting divorce. Instead, he directed people back toward a fulfillment of God's original purpose of marital permanence through a change of heart (10:2–12).

Thus Jesus reinterpreted Israel's central values: Promised Land, Jerusalem temple, and Mosaic law. He was aiming at a deeper liberation and restoration than expected—a renewal of people's hearts, so that they might become what God created them to be.

Jesus did not undertake a mission to non-Jews, but by shifting the focus of God's activity from the distinctive Jewish essentials of land, temple, and law, he opened the way for non-Jews to share in God's kingdom. On occasion he used his miraculous powers to aid non-Jews as well as Jews (7:24–8:10).

A kingdom now but not yet. Jews in the first century envisioned various scenarios regarding the last days. Generally, they did not expect the material universe to end. Rather, they thought God would transform the world and begin a new, final age of holiness and peace. By declaring that God's kingdom was about to arrive, Jesus indicated that this final age was dawning. Yet it was not descending from heaven with manifest power and glory but springing up mysteriously in small, seemingly insignificant ways (chapter 4). The final age of God's loving care for men and women was beginning, bringing forgiveness and healing and God's guiding Spirit, yet this did not mean the immediate end of suffering and persecution (8:34–38; 10:29–30). Unexpectedly, God's reign was both present and still to come.

A suffering messiah. Most surprising was Jesus' understanding of the chief task God had given him. Jesus shocked his followers by informing them that, in fulfillment of God's purposes, he was going to allow himself to be arrested, tortured, and executed by the religious and political authorities; after this, he would rise from the dead (8:31). While resurrection belonged to Jewish expectations of the final age, the humiliating death of the Messiah certainly did not.

How we can connect with the story. If Jesus had fulfilled God's promises according to Jewish expectations of the time, his life might not have had much meaning for us, since we are not Jews living in the land of Israel in the early first century. The meaning of Jesus' life for us lies in the unexpected way that he fulfilled God's promises. As we read Mark's Gospel, we will explore how Jesus' surprising fulfillment of God's promises to Israel is very good news for us. Before we begin, I would like to point out a couple of handles to grab hold of in your reading of Mark that may help you hear what God wishes to say to you through the Gospel.

The secret of Jesus' identity. Jesus evoked sharply different reactions—admiration and fear, faith and consternation. Because of his authoritative manner, the miracles that supported his claims, and the crowds that were drawn by his miracles, Jesus was difficult for people to ignore. They were forced to wrestle with the question of his identity (1:27; 6:2–3). Was he a nobody from nowhere, merely the carpenter of Nazareth, who was leading people astray from God's covenant with Israel? Or was he someone immeasurably greater? The men and women who became his disciples were not freed from this struggle to understand him. Far from it. They experienced firsthand the bafflement and terror of following a man who rejected earthly ambitions and regarded crucifixion as the capstone of his work (10:32–34).

Mark portrays Jesus as exercising his authority openly yet being secretive about his identity. Jesus sometimes commanded the people he healed not to spread reports about their healing (1:43–44; 5:43). He ordered evil spirits, who knew who he was, to be silent (1:34). He told his disciples not to broadcast their knowledge of him (8:30; 9:9). He referred to himself as "the Son of Man" (2:10, 28; 8:31), a term that would intrigue his listeners without giving them a clear answer to the question Who are you?

While Jesus bears various titles in Mark's Gospel—Messiah, king, son of David—the title that comes closest to expressing his fundamental identity is the title that most clearly expresses his relationship with God: Jesus is the "Son of God" (1:11). This is how God thinks of Jesus. Jesus kept this title secret, publicly affirming it only at his trial (14:61–62). Mark's Gospel is thus the drama of the revelation and recognition of Jesus as the Son of God. The dramatic interest lies in whether the people around Jesus will come to grasp who he is.

As readers of Mark *we* are in no suspense regarding Jesus' true identity. Mark tells us plainly at the outset that Jesus is God's Son (1:1). Early on, Mark lets us listen in as God declares Jesus' divine sonship at his baptism (1:11—a declaration not heard by any of the human bystanders). We watch the people around Jesus struggling to discover who he is, but we already know.

Ah, but do we? As we watch the people in the story stumbling around, failing for the most part to discover who Jesus really is, should we pat ourselves on the back for our superior insight? Or should we ask ourselves whether, for all our superior knowledge, we really know Jesus any better than the people in the Gospel? Mark invites us to enter into the drama of his Gospel by asking ourselves questions about how well *we* recognize Jesus. What, after all, does it mean to *know* Jesus, the Son of God? Does knowing him involve merely being informed of his title, or is it something more personal, more rewarding, more demanding? How well do I know Jesus? What does knowing Jesus mean for my life? If we keep these questions in mind as we read, Mark's Gospel will be an opportunity to grow in knowledge of Jesus at the level of experience and commitment.

The disciples' mediocre response. After Jesus began to preach, his first act was to call a handful of men to become his disciples (1:16–20). From then until the moment of his arrest, he was constantly surrounded by his followers, who included women as well as men (15:40–41). Jesus kept his disciples close to him and gave them special instructions and opportunities to share in his work (3:14; 4:10–11; 6:7–13).

At times, Jesus' disciples showed signs of understanding what he was about (8:29). They took steps toward genuine discipleship (1:16–20; 10:28). But it cannot be said that they set an example of how to follow him. Sometimes they seemed resistant to the truth about Jesus (8:14–21). They even attempted to stand in his way as he sought to carry out God's plans (8:32). In the end, when he was arrested, they embarrassed him by running away and even denying any relationship with him (14:50, 66–71).

Jesus of Nazareth, as Mark portrays him, was a man of intense personal magnetism, a man for whom men and women were willing to leave everything. The promise that he would bring Israel's hopes to fulfillment was deeply motivating to them. Yet it was not easy for them to follow this man who took such an unexpected path to the fulfillment of God's plans. Their attempts to follow him exposed their weaknesses. Their "first round" of discipleship—the round we see in Mark's Gospel—ended in failure.

Again, Mark invites us to enter into the story. He invites us to identify with the disciples in their initial responsiveness to Jesus and enthusiasm for his mission. That is how we would like to be! Then, when the disciples fail to understand Jesus, when they try to block him, when they abandon him, we are brought up short. We are forced to ask ourselves whether we have the tendencies these first disciples displayed. If these tendencies led the first disciples to abandon Jesus, where might the same tendencies lead us? If we recognize something of ourselves in the first disciples and do not like it, what are we going to do about it?

These are serious questions. But then, Mark relates a serious story. Only if we are serious about facing the deepest questions about God and ourselves are we ready to read Mark's Gospel. Only then will we perceive the surprisingly good news that it contains.

Are you serious?

THE KINGDOM OF GOD HAS COME NEAR

Questions to Begin

15 minutes
Use a question or two to get warmed up for the reading.

1 What's the most difficult change of diet you have ever had to make (when you left home, moved to college, traveled in a foreign country, experienced health problems)?

2 What's your approach to morning?
❏ I love to get up very early. (How early is that? What do you do then?)
❏ I'd like to get up early, but I rarely get to bed early enough to get up early. (What keeps you up at night?)
❏ I hold on to every last minute in bed.
❏ Please don't talk to me before ten o'clock.

Opening the Bible

5 minutes
Read the passage aloud. Let individuals take turns reading
paragraphs.

The Reading: Mark 1:1–39

The Advance Man

1 The beginning of the good news of Jesus Christ, the Son of God.
2 As it is written in the prophet Isaiah,
    "See, I am sending my messenger ahead of you,
        who will prepare your way;
    3 the voice of one crying out in the wilderness:
        'Prepare the way of the Lord,
        make his paths straight,'"
4 John the baptizer appeared in the wilderness, proclaiming a baptism
of repentance for the forgiveness of sins. 5 And people from the whole
Judean countryside and all the people of Jerusalem were going out to
him, and were baptized by him in the river Jordan, confessing their
sins. 6 Now John was clothed with camel's hair, with a leather belt
around his waist, and he ate locusts and wild honey. 7 He proclaimed,
"The one who is more powerful than I is coming after me; I am not
worthy to stoop down and untie the thong of his sandals. 8 I have
baptized you with water; but he will baptize you with the Holy Spirit."
    9 In those days Jesus came from Nazareth of Galilee and was
baptized by John in the Jordan. 10 And just as he was coming up out
of the water, he saw the heavens torn apart and the Spirit descending
like a dove on him. 11 And a voice came from heaven, "You are my
Son, the Beloved; with you I am well pleased."
    12 And the Spirit immediately drove him out into the wilder-
ness. 13 He was in the wilderness forty days, tempted by Satan; and he
was with the wild beasts; and the angels waited on him.
    14 Now after John was arrested, Jesus came to Galilee, pro-
claiming the good news of God, 15 and saying, "The time is fulfilled,
and the kingdom of God has come near; repent, and believe in the
good news."

A Day in the Life

16 As Jesus passed along the Sea of Galilee, he saw Simon and his
brother Andrew casting a net into the sea—for they were fishermen.
17 And Jesus said to them, "Follow me and I will make you fish for
people." 18 And immediately they left their nets and followed him.

[19] As he went a little farther, he saw James son of Zebedee and his brother John, who were in their boat mending the nets. [20] Immediately he called them; and they left their father Zebedee in the boat with the hired men, and followed him.

[21] They went to Capernaum; and when the sabbath came, he entered the synagogue and taught. [22] They were astounded at his teaching, for he taught them as one having authority, and not as the scribes. [23] Just then there was in their synagogue a man with an unclean spirit, [24] and he cried out, "What have you to do with us, Jesus of Nazareth? Have you come to destroy us? I know who you are, the Holy One of God." [25] But Jesus rebuked him, saying, "Be silent, and come out of him!" [26] And the unclean spirit, convulsing him and crying with a loud voice, came out of him. [27] They were all amazed, and they kept on asking one another, "What is this? A new teaching—with authority! He commands even the unclean spirits, and they obey him." [28] At once his fame began to spread throughout the surrounding region of Galilee.

[29] As soon as they left the synagogue, they entered the house of Simon and Andrew, with James and John. [30] Now Simon's mother-in-law was in bed with a fever, and they told him about her at once. [31] He came and took her by the hand and lifted her up. Then the fever left her, and she began to serve them.

[32] That evening, at sundown, they brought to him all who were sick or possessed with demons. [33] And the whole city was gathered around the door. [34] And he cured many who were sick with various diseases, and cast out many demons; and he would not permit the demons to speak, because they knew him.

[35] In the morning, while it was still very dark, he got up and went out to a deserted place, and there he prayed. [36] And Simon and his companions hunted for him. [37] When they found him, they said to him, "Everyone is searching for you." [38] He answered, "Let us go on to the neighboring towns, so that I may proclaim the message there also; for that is what I came out to do." [39] And he went throughout Galilee, proclaiming the message in their synagogues and casting out demons.

10 minutes
Choose questions according to your interest and time.

1 In verse 2, who seems to be speaking? Who is the "messenger"? Who is "you"?

2 Who speaks in verse 11?

3 What do verses 16 to 20, 29 to 30, and 35 to 38 suggest about the relationship between Jesus and his first followers? How well do his followers understand him?

4 What impression of Jesus do you get from the things he says and does in this reading?

A Guide to the Reading

If participants have not read this section already, read it aloud. Otherwise go on to "Questions for Application."

W ho is Jesus of Nazareth? Many of us would answer, "He is the Son of God." But what does that mean? And what does it mean for us? If Jesus is God's Son, he is an inexhaustible mystery, and being in a relationship with him is also an inexhaustible mystery. Mark writes his Gospel to help fellow Christians grasp more deeply the mystery of Jesus, "the Son of God" (1:1), and what it means to follow him.

John the Baptist is a man with a single-minded sense of urgency. He has stripped his life down to the bare necessities in order to focus on what he expects God to do (1:6–8). John's manner of life is an unspoken sermon. The message: If you want to prepare for God's action in your life, structure your life on the conviction that whatever God wants to do is the most important thing in the world. That involves facing up to your sins and seeking God's forgiveness (1:4).

John's ministry is the beginning of the good news of Jesus (1:1). John continues to stand at the beginning of the good news in each of our lives. John advises us that if we wish to experience Jesus' coming, we must put aside whatever sins or encumbrances hold us back from responding to God's grace.

Jesus' first public act is to be baptized by John (1:9). Immediately afterward, God declares that Jesus is his Son, sending the Holy Spirit to give him the authority to carry out his mission (1:10–11). Jesus' relationship with God is the basis of his ability to carry out his mission. Similarly, our relationship with God provides the basis for carrying out whatever mission God gives us.

Jesus returns to Galilee and announces that the moment of God's decisive action among human beings has come: "The kingdom of God has come near" (1:15). God is beginning to rule over men and women in a direct, liberating way. Jesus repeats John's call to repentance, but in light of God's action, the call now has a new shade of meaning. We might paraphrase it as "Stop thinking and acting as though God were inactive and far away. *God is on the move!* Make whatever changes are necessary to respond to him!"

The announcement that God's reign "has come near" has an already-almost quality. In one sense, God's kingdom is now arriving. In another sense, his kingdom is near but has not yet arrived. God's kingdom is visible but not yet fully visible. God is not immediately setting right all the wrongs in the world, so it takes faith to recognize his action. Thus Jesus calls people to *believe* in the good news of God's arriving, but still somewhat hidden, kingdom (1:15).

Before recounting any of Jesus' teaching or miracles, Mark tells us about the calling of the disciples. This action spotlights Jesus' central purpose. His efforts are directed toward gathering and training a group of followers and sharing his mission with them. This continues to be his purpose in our lives. He calls us to become his followers, a commitment that involves joining his other followers.

The fishermen that Jesus calls immediately leave their nets and boats—and even their father—and begin to walk along the lakeshore with him (1:16–20). Presumably they have heard Jesus' announcement of the kingdom, but they are responding not only to his message but also to his invitation to a personal relationship with him.

Mark's account of Jesus' sudden call to these men conveys a sense of Jesus' personal authority over men and women. The next episode further underlines Jesus' unique authority. People are amazed that Jesus teaches about God on his own authority rather than by referring to learned opinions, as other Jewish teachers did (1:21–22, 27). To give us a visual image of the power of Jesus' teaching, Mark describes Jesus' confrontation with an evil spirit that is afflicting a man—probably with illness (1:23–26). When Jesus speaks, people are changed!

Almost in passing, Mark mentions that Jesus heals Peter's mother-in-law (1:31). Far from being unimportant, this episode expresses the dynamic that lies at the heart of following Jesus—being called, being healed, and beginning to serve. The woman is obscure and her service seems insignificant, but that is exactly what makes her a sterling example of the response that Jesus is looking for.

Questions for Application

40 minutes
Choose questions according to your interest and time.

---

1 How has God helped you come to faith and openness to him? What can you learn from your experiences?

---

2 If you believed that God was about to intervene in your life, what would you do to prepare?

---

3 How has your baptism shaped your identity and relationship with God? How could you live your baptism more completely?

4 In what part of your life do you find it especially difficult to detect God's presence? If you were more confident that God wishes to bring his kingdom into that part of your life, how would you handle it differently?

5 What hidden service to other people is Jesus inviting you to provide at this point in your life?

"It is deadly to request that each person take a turn sharing. . . . Speaking 'in turn' destroys spontaneity and forces individuals to focus on themselves."

Loretta Girzaitis, *Guidebook for Bible Study*

Approach to Prayer

15 minutes
Use this approach—or create your own!

✦ Ask one person to read Mark
1:16–20 aloud and then repeat
it. Ask another person to read
this excerpt from a sermon by
John Henry Newman, a nine-
teenth-century English
theologian:

We do not understand that his
call is a thing which takes place
now. We think it took place in
the apostles' days; but we do not
believe in it, we do not look out
for it in our own case. We have
not eyes to see the Lord.

Take a few minutes for silent
reflection. Close the reflection
time with a short prayer such
as "Lord, help each of us hear
your call. Give us the grace to
respond to you." End with an
Our Father.

Saints in the Making

Touching

This section is a supplement for individual reading.

Jesus touched and healed a man suffering from leprosy (1:40–45). For this man, being touched by Jesus was doubly significant. His disease made him a social outcast. Jesus' touch not only brought him physical healing but also ended his isolation from other people.

Leprosy produces horrible deformities, and until modern times it was mistakenly thought to be very contagious. As a result, victims of leprosy were shunned, literally regarded as untouchable. But through the centuries, Christians have imitated Jesus by caring for men and women suffering from leprosy. For some, the simple act of touching a person with leprosy has been a life-changing experience. St. Francis of Assisi was one of these people. The sight of leprosy filled him with horror. If people suffering from the disease approached him, asking for a handout, Francis would give them a coin but avoid any physical contact. One day, however, when a man with leprosy came up to him, on a sudden inspiration Francis placed the coin in the man's hand and then bent down and kissed his fingers. It was a victory over self-protectiveness, which Francis followed up the next day by visiting the local hospital for leprosy victims. Later Francis wrote, "The Lord granted me to begin my conversion. As long as I lived in my sins, I felt very bitter to see the lepers. But the Lord took me among them, and I exercised mercy towards them."

In the 1980s, a Florida businessman, Ferdinand Mahfood, began to organize relief efforts for poor people in the Caribbean. "On my first visits to leprosariums," he wrote, "I shrank from touching anyone. The sight of so many bodies so ravaged by this terrible disease left me shaken and fearful. 'Jesus,' I prayed one day. 'I know you want me to love these sick people as you have loved them. Please help me to express your love by touching them.' It wasn't easy to shake hands with the next leprosy patient I encountered, but that was the turning point. Truly, God makes his grace well up inside us when we ask him to help us."

Whose pain are you afraid of? What suffering person are you reluctant to touch, to get close to? Will you let God help you to love?

Between Discussions

The first chapter of Mark creates a strong impression of God's initiative. God made plans long ago (reflected in the Old Testament prophecies—1:2–3) and is now putting them into operation. John's desert life and preaching repentance express an almost physical sense of anticipation of God's action. Jesus announces that God's kingdom is near, and he makes an immediate impact on the people he meets.

The coming of God's reign means that God is beginning to care for men and women in a new way. We, in turn, are called to respond to him in a new way. If God were uninvolved in human affairs, it might be enough merely to follow whatever general guidelines for living he laid down. But if God comes personally to free us from evil and reconcile us to him, we should answer with our whole being.

God's activity is not ghostly or vague. It has a visible, tangible focus: Jesus of Nazareth. Jesus is the point at which God is making himself present. Thus the way to say yes to God is to say yes to Jesus. Mark's simple account of the calling of the first disciples illustrates how this works. Jesus invites Peter, Andrew, James, and John to follow him; they put everything aside in order to do so. The episode is a kind of icon-in-action of God's initiative and man's response.

An aspect of Jesus' activity that may puzzle us involves his encounters with people troubled by "unclean spirits," or "demons" (see 1:23, 34). People at the time thought that many illnesses were due to these evil entities. While the Church continues to recognize the existence of the devil and evil spirits (see the *Catechism of the Catholic Church,* sections 391–395), it abandoned long ago the prescientific mentality that viewed demons as a major source of sickness. While we may not agree with the demon diagnosis of many first-century people, it is clear from Mark's account that Jesus actually frees people from physical and mental suffering. By doing so he shows that he exercises God's power over all evils, material and spiritual—including all the evils that we ourselves will ever face. His exorcisms signal that the final struggle between God and evil expected by many Jews in the end times has begun.

John the Baptist exhorts people to step into the Jordan River and receive a "baptism of repentance for the forgiveness of sins" (1:4). Through this baptism, people express their sorrow for sins and their expectation of God's forgiveness. This expectation leads us to suppose that forgiveness will be a major part of Jesus' activity, and indeed forgiveness quickly comes to the fore in the section of Mark that we skip on the way to our next reading.

Jesus heals a man of a skin disease that makes him ritually impure under the Jewish law (1:40–45). Since the disease is regarded as a symptom of guilt, Jesus' healing of it is a symbol of forgiveness. Then Jesus tells a paralyzed man that his sins are forgiven (2:5). Finally, Jesus calls into discipleship a man whose occupation involves unjust practices and accepts an invitation to dinner at the man's home with some of his colleagues in injustice (2:13–17). Simply by his presence at the meal, Jesus implicitly extends God's forgiveness to host and guests.

Only when Jesus' actions are seen against the background of Jewish expectations can we perceive their full meaning. Given Jewish hopes that God will liberate his whole people, Jesus' small-scale acts of forgiveness and healing are signals that a large-scale action of God is under way—an action that will have implications for the whole world. Yet Jesus exercises an authority that goes beyond Jewish expectations. Unlike the rabbis, who wait for students to come to them, Jesus calls disciples, as though he has the right to determine the direction of men's and women's lives. He overpowers the forces of evil. He cures diseases with a word or a touch—an expression of creative power. He does what only God has the authority to do: forgive sins. He restores people's relationship with God through his own friendship with them, bypassing the system of reconciling sinners through temple sacrifices. To the religious authorities, Jesus' behavior seems an infringement on the prerogatives of God and a threat to the Mosaic law and the temple in Jerusalem (2:7, 16). He is heading into conflict with these religious figures.

WHO IS THIS MAN?

Questions to Begin

15 minutes
Use a question or two to get warmed up for the reading.

1 What do you most enjoy doing on a day off?

2 Describe a situation in which you had trouble communicating something important to another person. What was the source of the problem? Did you overcome it?

Opening the Bible

5 minutes
Read the passage aloud. Let individuals take turns reading paragraphs. (If participants have not already read "What's Happened," read that aloud also. Otherwise skip it.)

What's Happened

Jesus has begun to come into conflict with some of the Jewish religious leaders. In the process of healing a paralyzed man, Jesus tells him that his sins are forgiven. "Why does this fellow speak in this way?" some of the religious leaders wonder. "It is blasphemy! Who can forgive sins but God alone?" (2:7). Jesus gives the religious leaders even more to wonder about when he goes on to speak and act as a friend and even a "physician" of sinners (2:13–17). An essential aspect of Jewish life in the first century—as still today—was keeping the Sabbath, the God-ordained rest on the last day of the week. Observing the Sabbath was seen as a crucial sign of loyalty to God and faithfulness to the people of Israel. Jews took different approaches to keeping the Sabbath, however, and sometimes criticized each other's approach. In our next reading, Jesus strides onto this theological battlefield and stakes out a unique position.

The Reading: Mark 2:23–3:35

Two Disputes

23 One sabbath he was going through the grainfields; and as they made their way his disciples began to pluck heads of grain. 24 The Pharisees said to him, "Look, why are they doing what is not lawful on the sabbath?" 25 And he said to them, "Have you never read what David did when he and his companions were hungry and in need of food? 26 He entered the house of God, when Abiathar was high priest, and ate the bread of the Presence, which it is not lawful for any but the priests to eat, and he gave some to his companions." 27 Then he said to them, "The sabbath was made for humankind, and not humankind for the sabbath; 28 so the Son of Man is lord even of the sabbath."
3:1 Again he entered the synagogue, and a man was there who had a withered hand. 2 They watched him to see whether he would cure him on the sabbath, so that they might accuse him. 3 And he said to the man who had the withered hand, "Come forward." 4 Then he said to them, "Is it lawful to do good or to do harm on the sabbath,

to save life or to kill?" But they were silent. [5] He looked around at them with anger; he was grieved at their hardness of heart and said to the man, "Stretch out your hand." He stretched it out, and his hand was restored. [6] The Pharisees went out and immediately conspired with the Herodians against him, how to destroy him.

Crowds, Followers, Opponents, and Family

[7] Jesus departed with his disciples to the sea, and a great multitude from Galilee followed him. . . . [9] He told his disciples to have a boat ready for him because of the crowd, so that they would not crush him; [10] for he had cured many, so that all who had diseases pressed upon him to touch him. . . .

[19] . . . Then he went home; [20] and the crowd came together again, so that they could not even eat. [21] When his family heard it, they went out to restrain him, for people were saying, "He has gone out of his mind." [22] And the scribes who came down from Jerusalem said, "He has Beelzebul, and by the ruler of the demons he casts out demons." [23] And he called them to him, and spoke to them in parables, "How can Satan cast out Satan? [24] If a kingdom is divided against itself, that kingdom cannot stand. [25] And if a house is divided against itself, that house will not be able to stand. [26] And if Satan has risen up against himself and is divided, he cannot stand, but his end has come. [27] But no one can enter a strong man's house and plunder his property without first tying up the strong man; then indeed the house can be plundered.

[28] "Truly I tell you, people will be forgiven for their sins and whatever blasphemies they utter; [29] but whoever blasphemes against the Holy Spirit can never have forgiveness, but is guilty of an eternal sin"—[30] for they had said, "He has an unclean spirit."

[31] Then his mother and his brothers came; and standing outside, they sent to him and called him. [32] A crowd was sitting around him; and they said to him, "Your mother and your brothers and sisters are outside, asking for you." [33] And he replied, "Who are my mother and my brothers?" [34] And looking at those who sat around him, he said, "Here are my mother and my brothers! [35] Whoever does the will of God is my brother and sister and mother."

10 minutes
Choose questions according to your interest and time.

1 Do Jesus' opponents question his *ability* to heal?

2 From 2:25–26 and 3:9–10, what picture do you get of Jesus' relationship with his disciples?

3 Who does *they* refer to in 3:20?

4 Why might there be no mention of Jesus' father in 3:31–35?

A Guide to the Reading

If participants have not read this section already, read it aloud. Otherwise go on to "Questions for Application."

Our reading begins with two incidents that at first seem only to concern disagreements over how to apply the Mosaic prohibition against working on the Sabbath (2:23–3:6). But a more fundamental issue is involved, which is why the disputes evoke such deep feelings (3:5–6).

As they walk beside a field, Jesus' disciples pull off heads of grain and eat the raw seeds. The poor are allowed to engage in this form of gleaning (Leviticus 19:9–10; 23:22). Apparently Jesus' followers are poor. It is the Sabbath, however, and some sharp-eyed religious leaders, perhaps also out for a Sabbath stroll, accuse Jesus of letting his disciples break the law against harvesting on the Sabbath (2:23–24).

Jesus does not agree with the Pharisees' interpretation of the Sabbath law. To embarrass them, he mentions an incident in the Bible in which a respected figure, King David, acted in violation of the Pharisees' interpretation (2:25–26). The David incident provides a precedent for a flexible application of the Mosaic law in order to meet the needs of hungry people.

But Jesus is doing more than arguing in favor of giving priority to human needs. He is also saying something about himself, for he implicitly compares himself with David, Israel's greatest king. Jesus' concluding remark contains a wordplay that implies he exercises authority over the Sabbath, one of Israel's basic institutions (a more literal translation of 2:27–28 reads, "The sabbath was made for man, not man for the sabbath; so the Son of Man is lord even of the sabbath").

The Pharisees also consider healing to be a form of work forbidden on the Sabbath (3:1–2). Jesus' challenge to them is puzzling at first (3:4). All Jews recognize that one should break the Sabbath rules in order to save human life. But a shriveled hand is not life threatening, so why does Jesus speak in terms of life and death?

The answer is that Jesus *does* consider the man to be in a life-or-death situation. The kingdom of God is coming into the world through Jesus' teaching and healing. For the man with the withered hand, meeting Jesus in the synagogue *is* a matter of life and death.

If he receives healing from Jesus, he enters a new, living relationship with God; to miss the opportunity would be a kind of death. Since God's life-giving reign over human beings is coming through Jesus, Jesus' activities take precedence over ordinary rules for keeping the Sabbath.

In both incidents, then, Jesus makes two points. First, Sabbath rules should be applied flexibly to meet pressing human needs. Second, Jesus is the agent of God's action in a way that takes precedence over other considerations. Significantly, the two points go together. Giving priority to people's needs and giving priority to Jesus go hand in hand.

Jesus' healings and his claim that he plays a unique role in God's plans evoke widely different reactions. Not surprisingly, his healing power attracts crowds (3:7–10, 20). Also not surprisingly, many religious leaders take a stand against him. The religious leaders realize that if he goes unopposed, he will bring about a readjustment in the whole structure of Judaism. Their commitment to the status quo as divinely sanctioned leads them to conclude that Jesus' powers come from the devil rather than from God (3:22).

In defense, Jesus argues that freeing people from the effects of demons demonstrates that he has overcome the demons' leader (3:27). Jesus may be referring to an initial victory over the devil in his temptation in the desert after his baptism (1:12–13). Moreover, Jesus insists, since he is the one through whom God is overcoming evil and offering forgiveness, to attribute his activity to the devil is to reject God's offer of reconciliation. God is willing to forgive whatever sins anyone commits (3:28—a statement that may give us hope in our darkest moments of guilt). But if we refuse the one through whom God offers forgiveness, we will remain alienated from God (3:29). The choice is ours.

Hearing that Jesus is deranged, some members of his family come to "restrain" him (3:20–21). In response, Jesus declares that his real family members are those who obey God by following his teaching (3:31–35). The picture of people sitting around a room and listening to Jesus is a simple but profound image of the Church, the continuing community of Jesus' followers.

Questions for Application

40 minutes
Choose questions according to your interest and time.

1 In what areas of your life do you need healing?

2 Where do you sense Jesus calling you to change something in your life in order to serve him in a new way? How does whatever Jesus wishes to do in your life take precedence over your usual pattern of activities, habits, and preferences?

3 Where are you giving higher priority to your own concerns than to the needs of other people? What message does today's reading have for you in this regard?

4 Do people who make a radical response to Jesus sometimes seem a little crazy? Why?

5 Do you take an individualistic approach to following Jesus, or do you follow him as one of the group of his disciples? How do you express your belonging to the community of Jesus' followers?

"Assume that personal information spoken within the group setting is private, unless you are specifically told otherwise. Don't talk about it elsewhere."

Christian Basics Bible Studies series

Approach to Prayer

15 minutes
Use this approach—or create your own!

✦   Ask someone to read Mark 3:7–10 aloud. After a minute of silence, invite anyone who wishes to pray a brief prayer for someone who is in need from sickness, bereavement, loneliness, financial difficulties, etc. Close the time of intercession by inviting someone to pray a short prayer, such as "Lord Jesus, we bring all of these people to you, trusting in your love for them. Meet their needs, Lord. Guide us in helping to meet their needs also." End with an Our Father.

Saints in the Making

Two Saints in the Making

This section is a supplement for individual reading.

J esus' remarkable cures were signs that God's reign was coming into the world. In every age of the Church, God has continued to provide such signs of the presence of his kingdom.

Some of these miracles occur in response to prayers to saints and through their intercession. At times, Christians ask someone who has not yet been declared a saint to intercede for them. A miraculous answer can be taken as evidence that the person is in heaven. In fact, in the process of canonization, the Catholic Church requires at least one miraculous healing through the potential saint's intercession. A striking example of such an answer to prayer involved a little Massachusetts girl named Teresia Benedicta McCarthy. Her parents named her after Edith Stein, a German Jew who became a Christian and entered the Carmelite order as Sister Teresa Benedicta of the Cross. Edith Stein perished with a trainload of other Jews and people of Jewish ancestry in the gas chamber at Auschwitz extermination camp in August 1942.

When Benedicta—as the little girl was known—was two years old, she swallowed a lethal dose of Tylenol. Within a couple of days, her liver swelled up to five times its normal size and stopped functioning. Her kidneys began to fail. She continued to breathe only with the help of a machine. While the medical team began a nationwide search for a liver to transplant, Benedicta's parents decided to pray to Edith Stein. They called a couple of dozen friends and asked them to do the same. Within days, Benedicta's liver and kidneys were functioning normally.

For a decade after this recovery, the medical records and other details were sifted by physicians and theologians in Massachusetts and Rome. Finally, in 1997 the Vatican announced that Benedicta's healing met the Church's stiff criteria for a miracle. By that time Benedicta was a healthy fourteen-year-old who had no recollection of her early brush with death. Since Benedicta's healing came after prayers for Edith Stein's intercession, the miracle fulfilled the requirement for her canonization. In October 1998, Pope John Paul II formally added Edith Stein to the list of saints recognized by the Church.

Between Discussions

The men and women who accepted Jesus' invitation to follow him must have been astonished at his claims about himself. Here was an ordinary man, the carpenter of a nearby village, who acted as though he exercised God's authority over human lives, over Jewish institutions, over evil spiritual powers. Judaism provided no expectation that God would act in such a way through a human agent; it furnished no category in which to classify Jesus. Yet it seemed clear to his disciples that the religious leaders were mistaken about Jesus (3:22). Surely it was not the devil but God who supplied Jesus' power, since Jesus did produce effects that one would expect from God's Spirit—reconciliation with God, personal wholeness, peace among men and women.

In the chapters we skip over (4:1–8:26), Mark portrays the disciples' struggle to understand who Jesus is. Mark tells how Jesus continues to demonstrate his message about the arrival of God's kingdom with acts of extraordinary power. He miraculously feeds thousands of hungry people. He cures diseases and calms a storm. He even raises someone from the dead. Meanwhile the disciples strain to grasp what Jesus is about. He seems to fulfill, and exceed, and depart from their expectations in ways that keep them constantly off balance. They feel drawn to Jesus yet baffled by him.

No doubt Jesus' disciples attempted to understand him in terms of Jewish expectations for how God would act toward Israel. Like many Jews of the time, Jesus' followers probably expected that God would grant forgiveness and reconciliation to his people Israel, gather the scattered members of his people, dwell among them more openly in the temple, and restore them as a nation, giving them prosperity, peace, and possession of their land.

Jesus' designation of twelve of his followers as an inner circle must have raised the disciples' hopes that Jesus was restoring Israel, which originally consisted of twelve tribes. Yet Jesus made no move to drive the occupying Romans out of the land of Israel. Significantly, he included in his inner circle both a former agent of the occupying power (Matthew, a former tax collector—see Matthew 9:9) and a former Jewish freedom fighter (Simon the

Canaanaean—the title means "zealot" or "holy warrior"). Jesus, it seems, was aiming at a profound reconciliation among people rather than a political and economic renaissance of Jewish life.

Many Jews thought that God's kingdom would sweep away all injustice and suffering and open an entirely new age. Jesus' healings and exorcisms and miraculous provisions of food would have appeared to some Jews as powerful confirmation that God's kingdom really was arriving. Yet Jesus taught his disciples that the new era of God's reign was beginning *amid* the present age of sin and injustice and sorrow, without completely replacing it. In his parables, he spoke of a kingdom that grows from small, seedlike beginnings, remains hidden for a time, then breaks into the open and bears fruit (chapter 4).

Mark shows that Jesus' disciples do not entirely fail to understand who he is and what he is about. They continue to share his life as they walk with him from town to town. When he sends them out to announce God's kingdom, they carry out their commission (6:7–13). Yet they do not grasp his full identity. Even after one of his most amazing displays of power, they fail to take his power into account, and we find Jesus asking them reproachfully, "Do you not yet understand?" (8:21).

At the end of the section of Mark that we are skipping over, Jesus performs an odd miracle. He heals a man of blindness (8:22–26—his first healing of blindness) in two stages. At first the man recovers his sight partially. Jesus then puts his hands on the man's eyes again, and his sight is fully restored. The story is symbolic of Jesus' relationship with his disciples. They too need a miracle of healing to see who Jesus is and what it means to follow him. They too will receive their sight in stages. The next stage will occur in the incident we are about to read.

TURNING POINT

Questions to Begin

15 minutes
Use a question or two to get warmed up for the reading.

1 Describe a conversation that had a crucial effect on your life.

2 How has your view of a person changed as you got to know him or her better? Compare your early impression of the person with your later picture.

5 minutes
Read the passage aloud. Let individuals take turns reading
paragraphs. (If participants have not already read "What's
Happened," read that aloud also. Otherwise skip it.)

What's Happened

Jesus has traveled with his disciples from place to place, mobbed
by people seeking healing for themselves or their loved ones. The
scope of his miracles has increased. He calms a storm (4:35–41).
He brings peace to a man driven wild by inner conflict (5:1–13; the
man is infested with a legion of demons, that is, six thousand
demons!). He raises a little girl from the dead (5:35–43). Twice he
feeds thousands of people with some fish and a few loaves of bread
(6:33–44; 8:1–10). Nevertheless, the religious leaders remain
unconvinced that he has been authorized by God (8:11–13).

The Reading: Mark 8:27–9:9

You Are the Messiah

27 Jesus went on with his disciples to the villages of Caesarea Philippi;
and on the way he asked his disciples, "Who do people say that I am?"
28 And they answered him, "John the Baptist; and others, Elijah; and
still others, one of the prophets." 29 He asked them, "But who do you
say that I am?" Peter answered him, "You are the Messiah." 30 And
he sternly ordered them not to tell anyone about him.

31 Then he began to teach them that the Son of Man must
undergo great suffering, and be rejected by the elders, the chief
priests, and the scribes, and be killed, and after three days rise again.
32 He said all this quite openly. And Peter took him aside and began
to rebuke him. 33 But turning and looking at his disciples, he rebuked
Peter and said, "Get behind me, Satan! For you are setting your mind
not on divine things but on human things."

34 He called the crowd with his disciples, and said to them,
"If any want to become my followers, let them deny themselves and
take up their cross and follow me. 35 For those who want to save their
life will lose it, and those who lose their life for my sake, and for the
sake of the gospel, will save it. 36 For what will it profit them to gain
the whole world and forfeit their life? 37 Indeed, what can they give in
return for their life? 38 Those who are ashamed of me and of my
words in this adulterous and sinful generation, of them the Son of

Man will also be ashamed when he comes in the glory of his Father with the holy angels." 9:1 And he said to them, "Truly I tell you, there are some standing here who will not taste death until they see that the kingdom of God has come with power."

This Is My Son

2 Six days later, Jesus took with him Peter and James and John, and led them up a high mountain apart, by themselves. And he was transfigured before them, 3 and his clothes became dazzling white, such as no one on earth could bleach them. 4 And there appeared to them Elijah with Moses, who were talking with Jesus. 5 Then Peter said to Jesus, "Rabbi, it is good for us to be here; let us make three dwellings, one for you, one for Moses, and one for Elijah." 6 He did not know what to say, for they were terrified. 7 Then a cloud overshadowed them, and from the cloud there came a voice, "This is my Son, the Beloved; listen to him!" 8 Suddenly when they looked around, they saw no one with them any more, but only Jesus.

9 As they were coming down the mountain, he ordered them to tell no one about what they had seen, until after the Son of Man had risen from the dead.

Questions for Careful Reading

10 minutes
Choose questions according to your interest and time.

1 How would you answer Jesus' question in 8:27? How would you explain your answer?

2 Why does Jesus speak so sharply to Peter?

3 How would you paraphrase what Jesus says to Peter about "setting your mind not on divine things but on human things" (8:33)?

4 What connection is there between 8:27 and 9:7?

A Guide to the Reading

If participants have not read this section already, read it aloud. Otherwise go on to "Questions for Application."

For some time Jesus' disciples have observed him at close range and have struggled to understand who he is. Now they have reached a conclusion: he is the agent designated by God to play the crucial role in the coming of God's kingdom—the Messiah (8:29; in Greek, the Christ).

Quite likely Jesus' disciples feel exhilarated at having completed the climb up the mountain of questions about his identity. They can now look forward to watching him bring Jewish national hopes to fulfillment. But they have only scaled the foothills of Jesus' identity and mission; the peaks lie ahead. As soon as Peter makes his pivotal declaration of Jesus' identity, Jesus commands his followers not to discuss it with anyone (8:30). While their understanding of him is correct as far as it goes, it does not go far enough. Jesus *is* the Messiah. But they do not yet grasp what kind of messiah he is. They do not yet know his full identity as Son of God or have any idea of the death by which he will accomplish his mission.

Up to this point, differences between Jesus' outlook and that of his disciples have lain hidden beneath the surface, although there have been subtle hints that he and his disciples have divergent views about his mission (1:35–38). But as soon as Jesus speaks about his approaching death (8:31), the differences explode into the open. Peter, who voiced the disciples' discovery of Jesus' identity (8:29), instantly expresses their objection to Jesus' plans (8:32).

Jesus rebukes Peter sharply. We might paraphrase his "Get behind me, Satan!" (8:33) as "Don't get in my way! If you're going to be my follower, then *follow* me!"

Yet Jesus' attitude toward his disciples is not harsh: he patiently teaches them (8:34–38). Being his disciple, Jesus says, involves a basic decision to deny yourself and give your life to him. This is often taken to mean that Jesus' disciples should deny themselves things. But Jesus calls his disciples not to deny themselves *things* but to deny *themselves.* A figure skater who denied herself alcohol or tobacco while in training in order to win a competition would not be a model of self-denial. She might very well be an example of self-denial, however, if she dropped out of competition in order to care for her sick mother.

Up to this point in Mark's Gospel, it has probably been easy for most of us to identify with Jesus' disciples. They, like us, are willing to follow Jesus, hopeful that their lives will be better for it. Do we now continue to see ourselves in the disciples? Do we recognize ourselves in their incomprehension of Jesus' plan to submit to a painful and humiliating death? Do we, like them, also think in an earthly way, rather than in the way God thinks (see 8:33)? Jesus calls his followers to live for life in the age to come, when Jesus "comes in the glory of his Father" (8:38). Are we willing to live for that?

After this conversation, Jesus begins a journey to Jerusalem, where, he knows, he will die. Unless the disciples change the way they are looking at things, they will not succeed in staying with him all the way to the cross. Do we also need conversion, if we are to continue with Jesus on the path in life on which he wishes to lead us?

It is not only Jesus' impending death but also his divine sonship that the disciples have not yet understood. His sonship now becomes the focus of an extraordinary revelation. Three of Jesus' closest followers are given a vision of him radiant with heavenly light, accompanied by the two greatest prophets of Israel. The vision reveals to the terrified disciples (9:6) that Jesus is much greater than they supposed. Jesus has puzzled friends, family, and foes by acting with an authority that seems to exceed the scope of any human agent of God. The voice of God now sounds forth, clarifying the reality that lies behind these hints of Jesus' true identity: Jesus is God's Son.

Significantly, this vision does not occur right after Peter acknowledges Jesus as Messiah; it happens only after Jesus explains the kind of messianic mission he is on and what it will require of his followers (8:31–38). Thus when God commands the disciples to pay attention to Jesus (9:7), he confirms Jesus' words about his death and about taking up one's cross to follow him.

Questions for Application

40 minutes
Choose questions according to your interest and time.

1   When have you had a moment
of coming to know Jesus in a
deeper way? What effect did it
have on you?

2   Describe a recent situation in
which you faced a choice about
denying yourself. What did you
do? What did you learn about
yourself?

3   What goals are you most intent
on achieving? How do you
relate those goals to Jesus'
words in 8:36?

4 God strengthens the disciples' faith in Jesus by giving them a vision of Jesus' divine glory. What particular persons or events have played a crucial role in building your faith in Jesus? What can you learn from these experiences about how you might strengthen the faith of other people?

5 God tells the disciples to listen to Jesus (9:7). What gets in the way of your listening to Jesus? What could you do to reduce the interference?

"The Bible can become for us the revealed word of God. It is God speaking to each of us personally, now."

James Rauner, *The Young Church in Action*

Approach to Prayer

15 minutes
Use this approach—or create your own!

✦ Pray an Our Father together. Invite a volunteer to pray aloud briefly for God's help in dying to self as a disciple of Jesus. Then let everyone pray together Psalm 89:15: "Happy are the people . . . who walk, O Lord, in the light of your countenance."

Ask someone to read Mark 9:2–8 aloud. Pause for silent reflection. Finally, ask someone to read this Eastern Christian prayer:

Before your crucifixion, O Lord, taking the disciples up into a high mountain, you were transfigured before them, shining on them with the bright beams of your power. From love of humankind you desired to show them the splendor of the resurrection. Grant that we too in peace may be counted worthy of this splendor, O God, for you are merciful and love humankind.

A Living Tradition

The Purpose of the Transfiguration

This section is a supplement for individual reading.

The following excerpt is from a sermon by St. John Chrysostom, fourth-century bishop of Constantinople (present-day Istanbul):

Jesus had spoken a great deal about dangers and death and had given directions regarding those harsh realities. He had instructed the disciples about the good things that were to be hoped for. For example, he said that he would come in the glory of his Father to give rewards. He wished also to show them, to the degree it was possible for them to grasp, the glory with which he is going to come. He revealed this to them so that they should not be distressed anymore concerning their own death or that of their Lord—especially grief-stricken Peter.

Ever since he had heard that Jesus had to go to Jerusalem and suffer, Peter had been in fear and trembling for him. After Jesus rebuked him, Peter did not dare come up to him again and try to dissuade him in the same way. But now, because of that fear, Peter aimed at the same thing indirectly. For when Peter saw the remoteness of the mountain and the wilderness, he got the idea that the location offered safety, and of course, there would be safety not only in staying at the location but also in canceling the trip to Jerusalem. So, wishing Jesus simply to stay there, Peter mentions dwellings. For, he thinks, if we build dwellings, we won't go up to Jerusalem, and he will not die. He doesn't dare say this directly, but wishing to prepare the way for this plan, he says cautiously, "Rabbi, it is good for us to be here." . . . And what does the voice say? "This is my Son, the Beloved." If he is the Beloved, do not fear, Peter! You should already have been fully confident of his power and his resurrection. But since you are not, take courage from the voice. For if God is powerful, as indeed he is, then clearly the Son is likewise powerful. So don't be afraid of terrifying things. He is the Son loved by the Father. If he is loved, do not fear. Although you love him ten thousand times over, you do not love him as his Father loves him. . . . Even if he wills to be crucified, do not stand in his way.

Between Discussions

Jesus' ministry and his dealings with his disciples now enter a new phase. Like the blind man healed at Bethsaida (8:22–26), they are beginning to see, but not all at once. They have recognized that Jesus is the Messiah. But they are only beginning to grasp Jesus' divine sonship and the demands of following him.

After the climactic conversation near Caesarea Philippi and the revelation on the mountain, Jesus begins a journey south to Jerusalem. On this trip Jesus' focus shifts. Up to now, his miracles have signaled the coming of the kingdom. Now he works fewer miracles and focuses instead on training his disciples in how to respond to the coming of God's kingdom. His kingdom is different than they expect and requires a different response than they are so far ready to give.

It is not long before Jesus returns to the subject of his approaching death (9:30–31). But his disciples obviously do not understand, for they immediately start arguing over which of them has the most important role in Jesus' plans (9:34). They have failed to grasp that living in God's kingdom revolves around love for other people rather than self-advancement (see 9:35–37).

After teaching about relationships among his followers and about marriage, children, and material resources (9:38–10:31), Jesus returns once more to the subject of his impending death and resurrection (10:32–34). Again, his disciples do not get it. Two of them immediately ask him to appoint them to the most important positions of authority in his kingdom (10:35–37). The two disciples address Jesus as "Teacher" (10:35). Yet rather than being shaped by his teaching, they wish to shape him to fulfill their desires. If they regarded Jesus as their teacher, they would affirm that they are willing to do whatever *he* asks.

In response, Jesus tells them that true greatness does not lie in having authority over people but in caring for them (10:42–44). Jesus uses a Greek word—translated "serve" in 10:45—that literally means "to wait on tables" (see Acts 6:2). He says that he himself is this kind of servant. Biblical scholar Ernest Best comments that it is "a simple and unimpressive word for service. . . . There is nothing grand, heroic or dramatic about this; it is ordinary, daily, obscure, unnoticed by others." The kind of service that Jesus refers to is so ordinary and obscure that it is easy to overlook the only person in Mark's Gospel besides Jesus who offers this kind of service: Peter's mother-in-law (1:31).

Jesus' words help answer an important question about how we can live as his disciples. Being a disciple of Jesus involves more than accepting a body of teaching or a set of values: a disciple of Jesus has heard an invitation to become his personal follower. Yet what can this mean for us, since it is impossible for us to literally follow Jesus as he travels from place to place?

The "territory" through which we can now follow Jesus is not Palestine but our own lives. We travel with him not from Caesarea Philippi to Jerusalem but from birth to death. How can we follow Jesus through this territory? How do we know which "roads" he is leading us on, where he wishes us to go, what he wishes us to do? We know that he calls us to die to ourselves and follow him, but how can we know concretely what that means in our particular circumstances?

Jesus' lesson about taking the place of least importance and giving unobtrusive, humble service provides a crucial part of the answer. Whichever particular path Jesus wishes to lead us on, it leads through humble service. Thus we will have the best chance of finding the right path for our lives, the path Jesus wishes us to walk with him, if we take advantage of opportunities to serve other people. Of course, this will not answer all our questions about what path we should take. But if we are actively serving other people, we will at least be moving in the right direction and can trust Jesus to help us discern his will more clearly and specifically.

Finally, Jesus heals another blind man (10:46–52). This man's sight is restored all at once. Unlike other people whom Jesus heals, this man becomes one of Jesus' disciples. The significance of this miracle is hard to miss. The disciples may still be blind to Jesus' path of humble service, death to self, and resurrection, but he has the power to open their eyes and enable them—and us—to follow him.

THE HOUR HAS COME

Questions to Begin

15 minutes
Use a question or two to get warmed up for the reading.

1 What is your favorite place to pray? Where do you feel most at peace?

2 What is the next important meal (holiday, family celebration, etc.) that you are looking forward to? What will you do to make it a happy occasion for those who share it with you?

5 minutes
Read the passage aloud. Let individuals take turns reading
paragraphs. (If participants have not already read "What's
Happened," read that aloud also. Otherwise skip it.)

What's Happened

Coming to Jerusalem, Jesus provokes the religious authorities by a dramatic action that symbolizes the end of the temple's usefulness. He further angers them with his teaching (11:15–19; 11:27–12:44).

As today, Jews in the first century gathered at Passover to share a meal celebrating the exodus—God's rescue of the Israelites from slavery in Egypt. In Jesus' day, Jews traveled to Jerusalem to have a sheep or a goat slaughtered in the temple and then to eat the festive meal in the holy city. Jesus and his disciples share this meal on the night before his death (14:12–25).

The Reading: Mark 14:17–50

The Final Meal

17 When it was evening, he came with the twelve. 18 And when they had taken their places and were eating, Jesus said, "Truly I tell you, one of you will betray me, one who is eating with me." 19 They began to be distressed and to say to him one after another, "Surely, not I?" 20 He said to them, "It is one of the twelve, one who is dipping bread into the bowl with me. 21 For the Son of Man goes as it is written of him, but woe to that one by whom the Son of Man is betrayed! It would have been better for that one not to have been born."

22 While they were eating, he took a loaf of bread, and after blessing it he broke it, gave it to them, and said, "Take; this is my body." 23 Then he took a cup, and after giving thanks he gave it to them, and all of them drank from it. 24 He said to them, "This is my blood of the covenant, which is poured out for many. 25 Truly I tell you, I will never again drink of the fruit of the vine until that day when I drink it new in the kingdom of God."

26 When they had sung the hymn, they went out to the Mount of Olives. 27 And Jesus said to them, "You will all become deserters; for it is written,

'I will strike the shepherd,
        and the sheep will be scattered.'

^{28} But after I am raised up, I will go before you to Galilee." ^{29} Peter said to him, "Even though all become deserters, I will not." ^{30} Jesus said to him, "Truly I tell you, this day, this very night, before the cock crows twice, you will deny me three times." ^{31} But he said vehemently, "Even though I must die with you, I will not deny you." And all of them said the same.

An Anguished Prayer

^{32} They went to a place called Gethsemane; and he said to his disciples, "Sit here while I pray." ^{33} He took with him Peter and James and John, and began to be distressed and agitated. ^{34} And he said to them, "I am deeply grieved, even to death; remain here, and keep awake." ^{35} And going a little farther, he threw himself on the ground and prayed that, if it were possible, the hour might pass from him. ^{36} He said, "Abba, Father, for you all things are possible; remove this cup from me; yet, not what I want, but what you want." ^{37} He came and found them sleeping; and he said to Peter, "Simon, are you asleep? Could you not keep awake one hour? ^{38} Keep awake and pray that you may not come into the time of trial; the spirit indeed is willing, but the flesh is weak." ^{39} And again he went away and prayed, saying the same words. ^{40} And once more he came and found them sleeping, for their eyes were very heavy; and they did not know what to say to him. ^{41} He came a third time and said to them, "Are you still sleeping and taking your rest? Enough! The hour has come; the Son of Man is betrayed into the hands of sinners. ^{42} Get up, let us be going. See, my betrayer is at hand."

^{43} Immediately, while he was still speaking, Judas, one of the twelve, arrived; and with him there was a crowd with swords and clubs, from the chief priests, the scribes, and the elders. ^{44} Now the betrayer had given them a sign, saying, "The one I will kiss is the man; arrest him and lead him away under guard." ^{45} So when he came, he went up to him at once and said, "Rabbi!" and kissed him. ^{46} Then they laid hands on him and arrested him. . . . ^{48} Then Jesus said to them, "Have you come out with swords and clubs to arrest me as though I were a bandit? ^{49} Day after day I was with you in the temple teaching, and you did not arrest me. But let the scriptures be fulfilled." ^{50} All of them deserted him and fled.

10 minutes
Choose questions according to your interest and time.

1 Looking at this reading, how would you describe Jesus' attitude toward his impending death?

2 What indications does Jesus give that he is acting in accord with God's plan?

3 In Gethsemane, Jesus keeps the same three disciples with him who saw him transfigured (9:2; 14:33). What might the significance of this be?

4 There is a lot of body language—gestures, postures— in this reading. How does it enrich the meaning?

A Guide to the Reading

If participants have not read this section already, read it aloud.
Otherwise go on to "Questions for Application."

During the Passover meal, Jesus takes bread and wine and shares them with his disciples as his own body and blood (14:22–24). By doing this, he links the meal with his death, showing the disciples that his death will be like the Passover: through it, God will bring liberation and life. The death he is about to undergo will, he says, create a "covenant" (14:24), restoring the broken relationship between God and human beings.

Jesus' blessing and sharing of the cup of wine at the Passover meal alludes to an earlier explanation of his death. Jesus had spoken of drinking a cup and of giving his life as a "ransom" (10:38–39, 45). Drinking a cup of wine is used in Scripture as a metaphor for suffering punishment for sins (Isaiah 51:17; Jeremiah 49:12; Ezekiel 23:31–34). Jesus meant that he would suffer the punishment of sins—not his own but others'—as a ransom. He would die so that others might live. In the Gospel of Matthew, Jesus makes the meaning clearer by saying that his blood is shed "for the forgiveness of sins" (Matthew 26:28). Nailed to a cross, Jesus will suffer the punishment that weighs on all who reject God's will and harden their hearts against his voice—his disciples, his family, his enemies, and us—so that they may be forgiven and changed.

Jesus believes that his death will bring God's kingdom without delay, as he indicates by his declaration "I will never again drink of the fruit of the vine until that day when I drink it new in the kingdom of God" (14:25).

When we celebrate the Eucharist, Jesus shares with us what he did in his final Passover meal and on the cross. Our sins are removed, and our relationship, our covenant, with God is renewed. We feast already in God's kingdom. For, while we obviously still await the complete coming of God's kingdom, it has already begun to arrive through Jesus' death and resurrection. We experience it in part as we sit at table with the risen Lord.

One of the men eating the Passover meal with Jesus has been plotting to betray him (14:18–21). Across town, other men celebrating the Passover will gather after their meal to arrest Jesus. Fully aware of all this, Jesus leads the singing of the traditional psalms to end the Passover meal (one includes the line "Precious in the sight of the Lord is the death of his faithful ones"—Psalm 116:15) and goes out to meet his enemies.

Along the way, Jesus tells his followers that they will soon abandon him (14:27). Peter grants that the other disciples may well do such a shameful thing (14:29). He is willing to believe that his fellow disciples are cowards—but he will not believe that he is. But Jesus knows Peter better than Peter does.

As usual, Jesus is realistic about his followers, not harsh. He looks beyond their upcoming failure and assures them of his resurrection (14:28). They will see him again. The Old Testament prophecy that Jesus quotes (14:27; Zechariah 13:7) reinforces the message that he is about to suffer the divine judgment for sins so that men and women may go free.

The garden of Gethsemane, on a hillside facing Jerusalem, is a place of decision for Jesus—and for the disciples. Jesus deliberately passes up his last chance to escape his enemies. His prayer gives us an idea of the inner struggle involved in the decision (14:36). The disciples have been warned that they are about to face a test of their loyalty to Jesus, yet they fail to turn to God for help (14:37, 40, 41). Biblical scholar Werner Kelber remarks, "Their natural sleepiness is but the outward manifestation of a nonphysical, religious blindness." They have heard Jesus' message of the suffering entailed in following him, but they have not accepted it.

Nevertheless, Jesus continues to associate his followers with himself, speaking in terms of "us" right up to the moment they run away from him (14:42). He does not close the door to friendship with him, no matter how long it takes us to respond.

For the first time since he began to preach, Jesus uses the Greek word that means "be at hand" or "come near," this time to describe the approach of his betrayer (14:42; see 1:15). God's kingdom will now indeed come, but in a way that no human being could have conceived: through his Son's arrest, rejection, torture, death, and resurrection.

Questions for Application

40 minutes
Choose questions according to your interest and time.

1 When have you felt like Jesus in Gethsemane? What happened then? What did you learn?

2 Describe an experience that helped you realize your weakness in obeying God and your need for his help. How has this experience affected you?

3 How do you relate to people who ignore your instructions or advice? How do you respond to friends when they let you down? What could you do to be more patient in such situations?

4 What picture of Jesus emerges from this reading? Cite specific points in the text. What should this picture of Jesus mean for your relationship with him?

5 In what ways do you need to "keep awake," as Jesus urges in 14:34?

6 What could you do to be more receptive to Jesus in the celebration of the Eucharist?

"The leader should allow the discussion to develop. Avoid pushing or rushing."

John Burke, O.P., *Beginners' Guide to Bible Sharing*

Approach to Prayer

15 minutes
Use this approach—or create your own!

+ Ask someone to read Mark 14:36 aloud. Invite anyone who wishes to pray a brief prayer for people who are in the midst of suffering of any sort. Then pray Psalm 13 together. Close by praying an Our Father.

A Living Tradition

The Patience and Wisdom of the Lord

This section is a supplement for individual reading.

These reflections on the reading are from Bede, an eighth-century English monk.

On the Last Supper. "And when they had taken their places and were eating, Jesus said, 'Truly I tell you, one of you will betray me, one who is eating with me'" (14:18). Jesus, who has foretold his suffering (8:31), now also foretells his betrayer. This gives the betrayer an opportunity to change his mind. Realizing that his thoughts and secret plans are known, he might change his mind about what he is about to do.

Jesus does not even specifically identify his betrayer, since if he were exposed, Judas might become even more shameless. Instead, Jesus unleashes the accusation into the group ("one of you will betray me"—14:18) so that the one who knows himself to be meant might change his mind.

"He said to them, 'It is one of the twelve, one who is dipping bread into the bowl with me'" (14:20). What remarkable patience the Lord has! He says, "One of you will betray me." Yet the betrayer continues in his evil, even though he is obviously found out. While the other disciples are saddened by Jesus' announcement and discuss it among themselves, Judas boldly continues eating. With the same shamelessness with which he is about to betray his master, he continues to put his hand in the bowl with him, faking a good conscience by his audacity.

On Gethsemane. "Watch and pray that you may not enter into temptation" (14:38). It is impossible for human beings not to be tempted. For this reason, when we say in the Lord's Prayer, "Do not lead us into temptation," we mean, "Do not lead us into temptation that we are unable to bear." We pray that God would give us the strength to bear up in temptation, not that he would prevent any temptation to befall us. Therefore Jesus does not say, "Stay awake and pray so that you will not be tempted," but "so that you will not *enter into* temptation," that is, "so that temptation will not get the better of you and drag you into its traps."

Between Discussions

In the spring of 1535, Thomas More, former chief administrator of the English government, sat in a cell in the royal prison called the Tower of London. Henry VIII had jailed him for publicly refusing to support Henry's claim that, as king, he had the authority to govern the Church in England. The two men were old friends, but Henry was not a monarch to be crossed. More had every reason to expect to be executed for insisting that the pope, not the king, was the head of the Church in England.

With death before him, More turned his thoughts to Jesus' preparations for suffering. Over several weeks More wrote a commentary on the Gospel accounts of Jesus in the garden of Gethsemane that he entitled *Concerning the Sorrow, Weariness, Fear, and Prayer of Christ before His Arrest*. More did not live to complete the work. The manuscript breaks off abruptly—probably on June 12, 1535, the day prison authorities removed his paper and pens. Less than a month later, More's head fell under the executioner's ax.

In his commentary, More pictured the moment when Jesus uttered the anguished words "I am deeply grieved, even to death" (14:34): "Jesus sensed that close at hand, indeed virtually present, were the treacherous betrayer, the implacable enemies, the chains, the false charges, the verbal abuse, the scourging, the thorns, the nails, the cross, and the awful tortures continuing without interruption hour after hour. In addition, the terror of his disciples, the ruin of the Jews, even the destruction of the scoundrel who betrayed him, and, finally, the inexpressible anguish of his beloved mother—all these tormented him. The storm of all these evils, rushing together like the ocean through broken dikes, flooded into his kind and gentle heart."

Why, More asked, did Jesus experience such fear, when he had taught his disciples not to be afraid (4:40; 6:50)? Why did he quail at the suffering that lay ahead of him (14:36) rather than set a "good example" of fearless bravery?

The answer, it seemed to More, is that Jesus' command not to be afraid hardly meant that his followers "should never in any way be afraid of a violent death. Rather they should not fear and flee a temporary kind of death in such a way that they would, by denying their faith, run into an eternal death." Since fear in the face of danger is prudent, More reasoned, Jesus' injunction against fear did not mean "never feel afraid" but "do not give way to fear out of lack of trust in God."

While we should resist the impulse to turn away from suffering when it must be borne, More declared, we should not feel guilty about our dread of it. "There is no guilt attached to the fear of death and pain. In fact, this fear is an affliction that Christ came to suffer, not to escape." Fear is part of the human condition that the Son of God came to share with us.

More noted that while some people are naturally brave, many of us are not. Knowing this, Jesus encourages us "by the example of his own anguish, his own sadness, his own weariness, and his own unequaled fear." More imagined Jesus saying to the fainthearted, "Take courage and do not lose hope. You are afraid; you are sad; you are stricken with weariness and agitated with fear of the torment that is cruelly directed toward you. Trust me. I have conquered the world, yet I was immeasurably more frightened, more saddened, more wearied, more terrified at the sight of such awful suffering approaching. Let the brave one rejoice to imitate a thousand courageous martyrs. But you, my timid and peace-loving little sheep, be content to have me as your only shepherd, to follow me as your leader. Since you do not have confidence in yourself, hope in me. Look, I am walking ahead of you on this frightening road."

For Thomas More in his prison cell, Jesus' fear and prayer in Gethsemane were immediately relevant. Unlike More, perhaps few of us will have to confront the choice between a painful death and disloyalty to Christ. But we all meet situations in which the opportunity—or even the obligation—of service entails suffering, as well as situations in which suffering is simply thrust upon us. When our path leads through Gethsemane, More encourages us to draw close to Jesus, whom we will find there.

MESSIAH AND SON OF GOD

Questions to Begin

15 minutes
Use a question or two to get warmed up for the reading.

1 When have you had a second chance in life? What did you do with it?

2 When have you discovered that a situation was quite different from the way it appeared to you at first? How did you adjust?

5 minutes
Read the passage aloud. Let individuals take turns reading
paragraphs.

The Reading: Mark 14:53–72

Jesus Declares His Identity

53 They took Jesus to the high priest; and all the chief priests, the elders, and the scribes were assembled. 54 Peter had followed him at a distance, right into the courtyard of the high priest; and he was sitting with the guards, warming himself at the fire. 55 Now the chief priests and the whole council were looking for testimony against Jesus to put him to death; but they found none. 56 For many gave false testimony against him, and their testimony did not agree. 57 Some stood up and gave false testimony against him, saying, 58 "We heard him say, 'I will destroy this temple that is made with hands, and in three days I will build another, not made with hands.'" 59 But even on this point their testimony did not agree. 60 Then the high priest stood up before them and asked Jesus, "Have you no answer? What is it that they testify against you?" 61 But he was silent and did not answer. Again the high priest asked him, "Are you the Messiah, the Son of the Blessed One?" 62 Jesus said, "I am; and
      'you will see the Son of Man
      seated at the right hand of the Power,'
      and 'coming with the clouds of heaven.'"
63 Then the high priest tore his clothes and said, "Why do we still need witnesses? 64 You have heard his blasphemy! What is your decision?" All of them condemned him as deserving death. 65 Some began to spit on him, to blindfold him, and to strike him, saying to him, "Prophesy!" The guards also took him over and beat him.

Peter Fails the Test

66 While Peter was below in the courtyard, one of the servant-girls of the high priest came by. 67 When she saw Peter warming himself, she stared at him and said, "You also were with Jesus, the man from Nazareth." 68 But he denied it, saying, "I do not know or understand what you are talking about." And he went out into the forecourt. Then the cock crowed. 69 And the servant-girl, on seeing him, began again to say to the bystanders, "This man is one of them." 70 But again he denied it. Then after a little while the bystanders again said to Peter, "Certainly you are one of them; for you are a Galilean."

[71] But he began to curse, and he swore an oath, "I do not know this man you are talking about." [72] At that moment the cock crowed for the second time. Then Peter remembered that Jesus had said to him, "Before the cock crows twice, you will deny me three times." And he broke down and wept.

Questions for Careful Reading

10 minutes
Choose questions according to your interest and time.

1 Mark sandwiches the account of Jesus' trial (14:55–65) between portions of the account of Peter's betrayal (14:54, 66–72). What does this technique highlight about Jesus and Peter?

2 Reread what Mark says about Peter (14:27–31, 33–41, 50, 54, 66–72). How would you describe Peter? What are his motivations? his strengths and weaknesses?

3 How would you explain the difference between Peter's self-confidence (14:29, 31) and his later performance (14:67–71)?

A Guide to the Reading

If participants have not read this section already, read it aloud.
Otherwise go on to "Questions for Application."

Never have participants in an event been so blind to what is really taking place. The religious leaders see Jesus as a fraud and a troublemaker. To them, his claim to be the Messiah and Son of God is so self-evidently false that simply provoking him to make the claim gains the evidence needed to convict him (14:61–63). They think that humiliating and executing him will prove the emptiness of his claims and put an end to his influence. Yet the claim is true. And it is precisely by suffering torture and execution for claiming to be the Messiah and Son of God that Jesus will carry out his mission as Messiah and Son on behalf of the human race.

False witnesses report that Jesus declared he would destroy and rebuild the temple (14:57–58). This testimony may be a garbled form of a statement that Jesus actually made about replacing the Jerusalem temple with a new temple—the community of his followers. The accusers do not realize that their accusation, by helping to bring about Jesus' death, will contribute to the fulfillment of his prediction. Jesus' death and resurrection will establish a new bond between God and human beings. The men and women drawn into this relationship will offer God a deeper, more intimate worship in the community of the Church, the temple.

Tormentors mock Jesus as a false prophet for foretelling his ultimate vindication and triumph (14:65; see 14:62)—at the very moment when Peter is fulfilling Jesus' prophecy of his betrayal (14:66–72; see 14:30). Biblical scholar John Paul Heil comments, "They do not see that precisely by spitting upon him, abusing him, and mocking his power to prophesy, they are ironically fulfilling God's plan as prophetically predicted by Jesus: 'And they will mock him, spit upon him, scourge him, and kill him, but after three days he will rise' (10:34). . . . The irony that Jesus' past prophecies are being fulfilled precisely through the derisive mockery of his powers to prophesy assures the reader of the future fulfillment of his prophecies to rise from the dead with power to form a new community of authentic worship."

Jesus is not the kind of messiah the religious leaders envision. His Father's plan to use his suffering and death is different from any conception they have of God's action in the world. They do not see things from God's perspective; they see from a limited, purely human perspective (like Peter—8:33). We too suffer this limited perspective whenever we fail to realize that God's kingdom comes through nonretaliation in the face of rejection, through suffering accepted in the service of others, through courageous speaking of the truth.

While people fail to perceive God's kingdom and, in their ignorance, even seek to destroy it, God outmaneuvers human hardheartedness to advance his purposes. By enduring the attacks of his enemies, Jesus opens the way for the coming of God's reign over human beings. Thus God's kingdom comes in a manner that is not only hidden but also profoundly contrary to human expectations, through the suffering of self-giving love. And in this way it continues to come into the world.

Meanwhile, Peter has come to the house where the interrogation is being conducted. His relationship with Jesus is coming unraveled now that it has become dangerous to be associated with Jesus: Peter follows "at a distance" (14:54). This man, who has had the privilege of being with Jesus, now denies that he was with him (3:14; 14:67–68). The man who considered himself bravest among Jesus' followers is too great a coward to acknowledge even belonging to the group (14:29, 70–71). The man who claimed to know who Jesus is protests that he does not know him (8:29; 14:71)—and, in a sense, he is right. Peter does not really know Jesus, the suffering Son of God, nor does he grasp the self-denial involved in following him.

The contrast between Jesus and Peter is striking. Jesus courageously affirms that he is God's Son, accepting the death that this declaration will bring. As biblical scholar Jack D. Kingsbury puts it, "Jesus is taking a public stand at his trial on God's understanding of him. In saying 'I am' to the high priest, Jesus is daring to 'think' about himself the way God 'thinks' about him" (1:11; 14:61–62). Peter, however, is too afraid to acknowledge who he is—a disciple of Jesus. In denying Jesus, Peter also denies himself.

Questions for Application

40 minutes
Choose questions according to your interest and time.

---

1 What is the connection between Peter's behavior in Gethsemane (14:37, 40–41) and his behavior in the priest's courtyard (14:66–72)? What can you learn from this connection?

---

2 Peter is afraid to stay close to Jesus in his time of danger and suffering, so he only follows at a distance. Think of someone you know who is going through a time of difficulty. Do you avoid that person? How could you show loyalty and care for them in their suffering?

3 When do you find it most difficult to be identified as a Christian? How do you handle this situation? How might you handle it differently?

4 Jesus based his life on who he was in God's eyes—his Son. Who are you in God's eyes? How will that knowledge shape the way you live this week?

"Groups and the Bible and the way the Spirit brings them together can be more creative than the most carefully crafted study guide."

Dan Williams, *Starting (& Ending) a Small Group*

Approach to Prayer

15 minutes
Use this approach—or create your own!

✦ Take time to pray for each other's needs. Begin by praying Psalm 4 together. Invite participants to mention briefly a need in their own life or someone else's. After each need, invite a volunteer to pray a short prayer for the need mentioned. End by praying the Our Father together.

Saints in the Making

Are You One of This Man's Followers?

This section is a supplement for individual reading.

The servant came up to Peter in the courtyard and made a simple observation: "You also were with Jesus, the man from Nazareth" (14:67). She was not asking Peter for a lengthy account of Jesus' ministry or a detailed proof that Jesus was the Messiah. The servant was not asking Peter anything about Jesus. She was merely challenging Peter to confirm something about himself, something she was already pretty sure of— that Peter was a follower of Jesus. "That's right" would have been an entirely adequate response.

From time to time, we too face situations in which we must affirm that we are followers of Jesus. It may be a matter of stating our belief in him or making a moral decision or adopting a course of action we know is right. Despite whatever gray areas and complexities the situation may present, we face a basic choice, the same choice Peter faced: are we willing to speak and act in a way that clearly acknowledges our relationship with Jesus?

A person who thinks he is well equipped to live out his commitment to Jesus, like Peter, may unexpectedly lose his nerve when such a situation suddenly arises. On the other hand, a person who may not have seen herself as a potential hero of the faith may rise to the occasion. Without warning, in the middle of a school day in May 1999 in Littleton, Colorado, high schoolers were faced with two fellow students rampaging through the school, shooting almost at random. According to reports, in the course of the shooting spree one attacker pointed a gun at Cassie Bernall and Rachel Scott and asked, "Do you believe in God?" Undoubtedly it took the two high school girls only an instant to realize that yes was not a safe answer. But they said yes, and they were killed.

Of course, we rarely face such life-threatening situations. Our choices usually involve far less severe consequences. But in one way or another, all of us encounter challenges to affirm our relationship with Jesus. The example of people like Peter, Cassie Bernall, and Rachel Scott leads us to examine ourselves and to reflect on the meaning of passages such as Mark 13:9–11, 14:26–31, and 14:37–41.

Between Discussions

In our final excerpt from Mark, we will read about Jesus' death. As we all know, Jesus died on a cross. But Mark says little about the actual manner of Jesus' death (see 15:24), partly because it was shameful, partly because his readers did not need a description. Crucifixion was far from unusual in the Roman Empire, and it was always carried out in public. Consequently, many people had the opportunity to see crucifixion for themselves.

Most of us have formed our notion of crucifixion from representations of Jesus' death in religious art. Paintings, crucifixes, icons, and other representations portray Jesus' crucifixion in a variety of ways. They have something in common with Mark: they generally refrain from inflicting on the viewer the awful details.

Since Mark and the other New Testament writers are reticent about the particulars of Jesus' death, there is no way to construct a detailed account of it. But on the basis of ancient writings and archaeological discoveries, it is possible to get a picture of crucifixion that aids our reading of Mark.

In the first-century Roman world, crucifixion was considered the worst form of execution because it was extremely painful and often very slow. The victim was attached to a board or a stake, with or without a crosspiece, usually by nails through the feet and wrists (not through the hands, for the hands would pull loose of the nails). The atrocious pain of the body's weight bearing down on the nails was constantly intensified as the victim attempted to pull himself—or herself—up in order to breathe. Since no vital organs were directly involved, the crucified person might suffer for days before expiring from dehydration and asphyxiation. A peg was sometimes supplied as a seat that enabled the victim to continue breathing, thereby prolonging the agony.

Usually the victim was flogged before being nailed to the cross. Often this punishment was a scourging—a lashing with whips tipped with bits of metal. The ferocity of scourging can be judged from the fact that some victims died from it. Such torture could hardly be called merciful, but by weakening the victim, it could shorten the time he would suffer on the cross before dying.

Crucifixion was designed as a deterrent and so was carried out where people could see it. The Romans crucified their victims along roads or, if they were besieging a city, outside the city walls as a message to the defenders about what awaited them if they did not surrender immediately.

Numerous details in the Gospel accounts of Jesus' death fit with the historical evidence concerning crucifixion. Mark tells us that when the execution squad led Jesus out to the place of crucifixion, they forced a man named Simon to carry the cross (15:20–21). It was common to make the victim himself carry the crosspiece to the place of execution. Apparently Jesus' scourging had been so severe, however, that he was too weak to do this. After Jesus' death, a member of the Jewish ruling council asked Pilate for Jesus' body for burial. Pilate was surprised that Jesus was dead so soon (15:44). His surprise fits with the picture that emerges from historical sources of crucifixion as a usually prolonged agony, and it strengthens the conclusion that Jesus' scourging was especially terrible, bringing about a relatively rapid death.

Mark reports that "those who passed by" mocked Jesus (15:29). Jesus' cross was not set up on a lonely hill—as religious artists have sometimes imagined—but along one of the roads into Jerusalem, probably just outside one of the city gates. The crucified person, stripped of all clothing and hanging in agony, was a very public spectacle of utter humiliation.

The Gospel writer John reports that since Jesus was already dead, the soldiers did not break his legs, although they broke the legs of the other men crucified beside him (John 19:31–33). The practice of speeding up the crucified victim's death by breaking his legs, making it impossible for him to breathe, was illustrated by the 1968 discovery of the bones of a young Jewish man who had been crucified near Jerusalem in the first century. His lower leg bones had been shattered, apparently, in the view of the archaeologists and a medical examiner, in the manner that John describes in his Gospel.

THE RANSOM IS GIVEN

Questions to Begin

15 minutes
Use a question or two to get warmed up for the reading.

1   In your experience, when is silence the best response to critical or accusatory remarks?

2   When have you been especially glad to have finished a project or a stage of life?

5 minutes
Read the passage aloud. Let individuals take turns reading
paragraphs.

The Reading: Mark 15:1–41

Crucify Him!

[1] As soon as it was morning, the chief priests held a consultation with the elders and scribes and the whole council. They bound Jesus, led him away, and handed him over to Pilate. [2] Pilate asked him, "Are you the King of the Jews?" He answered him, "You say so." [3] Then the chief priests accused him of many things. [4] Pilate asked him again, "Have you no answer? See how many charges they bring against you." [5] But Jesus made no further reply, so that Pilate was amazed.

[6] Now at the festival he used to release a prisoner for them, anyone for whom they asked. [7] Now a man called Barabbas was in prison with the rebels who had committed murder during the insurrection. [8] So the crowd came and began to ask Pilate to do for them according to his custom. [9] Then he answered them, "Do you want me to release for you the King of the Jews?" [10] For he realized that it was out of jealousy that the chief priests had handed him over. [11] But the chief priests stirred up the crowd to have him release Barabbas for them instead. [12] Pilate spoke to them again, "Then what do you wish me to do with the man you call the King of the Jews?" [13] They shouted back, "Crucify him!" [14] Pilate asked them, "Why, what evil has he done?" But they shouted all the more, "Crucify him!" [15] So Pilate, wishing to satisfy the crowd, released Barabbas for them; and after flogging Jesus, he handed him over to be crucified.

My God, My God!

[16] Then the soldiers led him into the courtyard of the palace (that is, the governor's headquarters); and they called together the whole cohort. [17] And they clothed him in a purple cloak; and after twisting some thorns into a crown, they put it on him. [18] And they began saluting him, "Hail, King of the Jews!" [19] They struck his head with a reed, spat upon him, and knelt down in homage to him. [20] After mocking him, they stripped him of the purple cloak and put his own clothes on him. Then they led him out to crucify him.

[21] They compelled a passer-by, who was coming in from the country, to carry his cross; it was Simon of Cyrene, the father of Alexander and Rufus. [22] Then they brought Jesus to the place called

Golgotha (which means the place of a skull). 23 And they offered him wine mixed with myrrh; but he did not take it. 24 And they crucified him, and divided his clothes among them, casting lots to decide what each should take.

25 It was nine o'clock in the morning when they crucified him. 26 The inscription of the charge against him read, "The King of the Jews." 27 And with him they crucified two bandits, one on his right and one on his left. 29 Those who passed by derided him, shaking their heads and saying, "Aha! You who would destroy the temple and build it in three days, 30 save yourself, and come down from the cross!" 31 In the same way the chief priests, along with the scribes, were also mocking him among themselves and saying, "He saved others; he cannot save himself. 32 Let the Messiah, the King of Israel, come down from the cross now, so that we may see and believe." Those who were crucified with him also taunted him.

33 When it was noon, darkness came over the whole land until three in the afternoon. 34 At three o'clock Jesus cried out with a loud voice, "Eloi, Eloi, lema sabachthani?" which means, "My God, my God, why have you forsaken me?" 35 When some of the bystanders heard it, they said, "Listen, he is calling for Elijah." 36 And someone ran, filled a sponge with sour wine, put it on a stick, and gave it to him to drink, saying, "Wait, let us see whether Elijah will come to take him down." 37 Then Jesus gave a loud cry and breathed his last. 38 And the curtain of the temple was torn in two, from top to bottom. 39 Now when the centurion, who stood facing him, saw that in this way he breathed his last, he said, "Truly this man was God's Son!"

40 There were also women looking on from a distance; among them were Mary Magdalene, and Mary the mother of James the younger and of Joses, and Salome. 41 These used to follow him and provided for him when he was in Galilee; and there were many other women who had come up with him to Jerusalem.

Questions for Careful Reading

10 minutes
Choose questions according to your interest and time.

1   Does Pilate really think that Jesus is a threat to the Roman government?

2   Is Pilate a strong person?

3   What might be the symbolism of the roles played by Barabbas and Simon of Cyrene?

4   Why is it only Jesus' death, rather than any of his miracles, that finally leads someone to recognize him as God's Son?

A Guide to the Reading

*If participants have not read this section already, read it aloud.
Otherwise go on to "Questions for Application."*

After agreeing that Jesus must die, the Jewish leaders take him to the Roman governor Pontius Pilate, who exercises supreme judicial authority in the region. Their disagreements with Jesus concern religious matters, which would be of no importance to Pilate, but they make an accusation that is sure to get his attention. They charge Jesus with claiming to be the king of the Jews (see 15:2).

Pilate interprets the title *king* to mean that Jesus wishes to overthrow the Roman occupation and set up a Jewish kingdom. Jesus does see himself as king, but he intends to establish his reign not on a battlefield but on a cross. So he makes only a noncommittal reply to Pilate's question (15:2).

Once the term *king* is introduced, it rains down mercilessly on Jesus. Pilate sarcastically refers to him as "the King of the Jews" and puts that title above Jesus' head as the reason for his execution (15:12, 26). The soldiers entertain themselves by dressing Jesus up as a king and bowing to him (15:16–19). As Jesus hangs gasping on the cross, some of the priests, presumably within earshot, say to each other, "Let the Messiah, the King of Israel, come down from the cross now, so that we may see and believe" (15:32). Those who derisively call Jesus king are blind to his real kingship. They are blind to the mystery that their mockery of his kingship contributes to the coming of his kingdom.

The mysterious transaction at the cross is symbolized by the darkness that fills the sky (15:33). The darkness is a sign that judgment is taking place. God is bringing judgment on human hardheartedness and sin, but the judgment is suffered by Jesus rather than by sinners. Jesus said that he would give his life as a ransom (10:45). On the cross he endures the judgment that falls on those who reject God, so that we might go free. Jesus suffers God's judgment of sin (14:36) so that we, who would otherwise have had to suffer it, may instead experience God's merciful, caring, transforming rule (his "kingdom"—1:15) and live with God in a new bond of love (a new "covenant"—14:24). On the cross, Jesus drinks the cup of judgment so that we might drink the cup of salvation (10:38–39, 45; 14:23–25).

In the darkness and pain of judgment, Jesus cries out the first line of Psalm 22: "My God, my God, why have you forsaken me?" (15:34). As far as any human eyes can see, including his own, God has abandoned him. Jesus has not sinned, but he experiences the estrangement from God that falls as a judgment on sinners. His enemies' mockery only deepens his experience of alienation from God, adding humiliation to his physical pain.

The psalm that Jesus begins to pray continues, after an expression of agony, with a declaration of confidence that God will come to save (Psalm 22:22–31). As he dies, Jesus experiences the utter abandonment of God, the estrangement caused by sin, yet his praying Psalm 22 suggests that he continues to trust God, to cling to him as "my God."

Jesus dies for the disciples who have abandoned him, for the crowds who have rejected him, for the Romans who are executing him, even for the priests who stroll past his cross, mocking his kingship. The Greek word translated "derided" (15:29) is the same Greek word translated "blaspheme" in the earlier passage in which Jesus declared that God is willing to forgive every sin and *blasphemy* (3:28–29). Even those who condemn Jesus to death may be forgiven; indeed, it is Jesus' death that makes God's forgiveness available. No sin we could ever commit is beyond the range of the forgiveness accomplished at the cross.

Jesus breathes his last. Then, remarkably, the soldier in charge of the execution squad exclaims, "Truly this man was God's Son!" (15:39). It is the first time in the Gospel that any human recognizes and acknowledges that Jesus is God's Son. By his death, Jesus has given himself entirely to God's purposes, at the greatest possible cost to himself. Thus he has demonstrated his relationship with God more clearly than he could have in any other way. At the heart of Jesus' sonship is obedience to and trust in his Father. The obedience and trust manifest in Jesus' manner of death has brought the soldier across the chasm separating the human way of thinking from God's way of thinking. Through witnessing Jesus' death, the soldier has received the grace to perceive who Jesus is. God wants to give that grace to every one of us.

Questions for Application

40 minutes
Choose questions according to your interest and time.

1 When have you felt abandoned by God? What effect did this experience have on you?

2 When have you seen someone demonstrate patience, love, and trust in God in the midst of suffering? How were you affected by this person?

3 How might God use some present difficulty or suffering in your life for some good purpose? What might this reading say to you about this question?

4 How has reading Mark altered your picture of Jesus? How will this perception change your relationship with him?

5 How does the life and death of Jesus affect your life today? How does it affect decisions you are facing?

"In my opinion, it's better to cover three verses in depth, including application, than to force yourself to accomplish a specific goal and get through a certain amount of material."

Neal F. McBride, *How to Lead Small Groups*

Approach to Prayer

15 minutes
Use this approach—or create your own!

✦ Begin with an Our Father. Invite someone to read Mark 15:16–39 aloud, one paragraph at a time (verses 16–20, 21–24, 25–32, 33–39). After each paragraph, pray together, "We adore you, O Christ, and we praise you, because by your holy cross you have redeemed the world" and then pause for a minute or two of silent reflection.

At the end pray this ancient prayer:

Soul of Christ, sanctify me.
Body of Christ, save me.
Blood of Christ, inebriate me.
Water from the side of Christ,
    wash me.
Passion of Christ, strengthen me.
O good Jesus, hear me;
Within your wounds hide me;
Let me not be separated from
    you;
From the evil enemy defend me;
In the hour of my death call me
And bid me come to you,
So that with your saints I may
    praise you
Forever and ever. Amen.

A Living Tradition

On Contemplating Jesus on the Cross

This section is a supplement for individual reading.

I was utterly distressed in seeing him that way, for it well represented what he suffered for us. I felt so keenly aware of how poorly I thanked him for those wounds that my heart broke.

St. Teresa of Ávila, sixteenth-century Spanish mystic, after looking at a statue that depicted Jesus in his agony

Generously you dispossessed yourself. You took the nature of a slave, fashioned in the likeness of man and presenting yourself to us in human form. You lowered your own dignity, accepted an obedience which brought you to death, death on a cross.

You followed man in his remoteness from God. Your humility descended into the lost depths and brought us back. Therefore God has raised you to such a height, has given you that name which is greater than any other name; so that everything in heaven and on earth must bend the knee before the name of Jesus, and every tongue must confess Jesus Christ as the Lord.

And therefore I, too, bend my knee in your name, O Lord, and confess: you are the Lord, the redeemer and bringer of salvation.

Sin is blindness: and so I beseech you, my redeemer, rid me of the error of arrogance. Teach me to see who I am and who you are. Move my heart that it may feel what you have done.

In the hour when you changed our fate, O Lord, you were quite alone. No one was with you; there was no comprehension and no love. Alone you carried our guilt before God's justice. But now you have taken us up in your redemption, and I beseech you to grant that I may know you and be with you with my love.

Prayer of Romano Guardini, twentieth-century German theologian

A Surprise Ending

Mark Leaves Us with Questions

At his last meal, Jesus gave his followers an insight into the meaning of the death that awaited him. He was going to his death in obedience to God, whose plan was reflected in Scripture: "The Son of Man goes as it is written of him," Jesus said (14:21). With gesture and interpretation, Jesus showed that his death would create a new relationship between God and human beings: "He took a cup, and after giving thanks he gave it to them, and all of them drank from it. He said to them, 'This is my blood of the covenant, which is poured out for many'" (14:23–24). Jesus signaled his expectation that his death would bring God's kingdom, for he implied that he would eat his next meal with his followers in the kingdom: "Truly I tell you, I will never again drink of the fruit of the vine until that day when I drink it new in the kingdom of God" (14:25).

In the brief conclusion of his Gospel, Mark assures us that these expectations have begun to be fulfilled. Jesus has completed his surprising announcement of God's kingdom with an utterly unparalleled surprise: after dying, he has risen from the dead. Through his death and resurrection, he has accomplished all that he promised.

While Jesus' resurrection is *the* great surprise at the end of Mark's Gospel, the ending is surprising in other respects also. In order to see this, it is necessary to recognize a distinction between Mark's ending and the ending of Mark. Mark's ending, that is, the ending that Mark himself wrote, is 16:1–8. The longer ending, 16:9–20, seems to have been added by an early editor of the Gospel. The Church recognizes the longer ending as inspired Scripture; it belongs to the canon of the New Testament as much as the rest of Mark does. But to grasp the message that Mark himself wished to communicate, we should pay close attention to the way he brought his account to a close. Mark's own ending, which seems abrupt, has something to teach us.

1 When the sabbath was over, Mary Magdalene, and Mary the mother of James, and Salome bought spices, so that they might go and anoint him. 2 And very early on the first day of the week, when the sun had risen, they went to the tomb. 3 They had been saying to one another,

"Who will roll away the stone for us from the entrance to the tomb?" ⁴ When they looked up, they saw that the stone, which was very large, had already been rolled back. ⁵ As they entered the tomb, they saw a young man, dressed in a white robe, sitting on the right side; and they were alarmed. ⁶ But he said to them, "Do not be alarmed; you are looking for Jesus of Nazareth, who was crucified. He has been raised; he is not here. Look, there is the place they laid him. ⁷ But go, tell his disciples and Peter that he is going ahead of you to Galilee; there you will see him, just as he told you." ⁸ So they went out and fled from the tomb, for terror and amazement had seized them; and they said nothing to anyone, for they were afraid.

Two remarkable features of this account are the presence of the women and the absence of Jesus.

The women had stood at a distance from Jesus' cross (15:40). Some scholars argue that these women may have been with Jesus and the male disciples at the Last Supper. Mark does not mention women at the meal, but it was normal for women to share the Passover meal with men, so we cannot conclude anything from Mark's silence on the matter. We do know that many women had accompanied Jesus to Jerusalem for the festival (15:41), and there would have been room for at least some of them at the meal, for Jesus had arranged for a large room (14:15). In any case, a few women had watched him die and had also witnessed his burial (15:47).

In Mark's conclusion, the women come to the tomb two days after Jesus' death, intending to honor him by placing aromatic spices in the wrappings around his body (16:1). While these women have shown more loyalty to Jesus than his male followers, they seem utterly unprepared for what they discover at the tomb (16:5). The announcement of Jesus' resurrection breaks upon them as a terrifying revelation (16:8). Now it is their turn to run away (16:8; compare 14:50).

Evidently the women do eventually report on what they found at the tomb (as the later editor confirms in 16:10). And when they do, the fact that they were not expecting Jesus to rise from the dead will make their testimony particularly credible. The angel was hardly a figment of hopeful imaginations.

Indeed, the women's very presence in Mark's account is a strong indicator of its factual basis. Women were not considered competent to offer legal testimony. Thus, if anyone were to try to lend credibility to fiction, he would hardly invent a group of female witnesses.

As to Mark's "failure" to provide an account of the risen Jesus, it may not have seemed as strange to his first readers as it does to us. Scholars think it quite possible that Mark's was the first Gospel to be written. In this case, his readers did not have the other three Gospels to compare it with. Unlike us, then, Mark's first readers would not expect that a Gospel *should* end with a description of Jesus after his resurrection (compare Matthew 28:9–10, 16–20; Mark 16:12–18; Luke 24; John 20–21).

We must conclude that Mark viewed his brief account of the empty tomb as sufficient to serve his purposes. He wished to show that Jesus' ransoming, covenant-making death (see 10:45; 14:24) achieved its goal. The empty tomb and the angel's announcement that Jesus has risen from the dead confirmed that Jesus achieved his objective. Jesus now lives as God's Son in the glory of his kingdom. The reconciliation with God that lies at the heart of God's kingdom is available to all. God's reign over men and women, which Jesus proclaimed to be near, has now arrived.

This is not to say that Mark thought God's kingdom had ceased to be a somewhat hidden, even paradoxical, reality. As it was during Jesus' earthly life, God's reign is still now-but-not-yet-fully-now. The complete coming of the kingdom lies ahead of us at Jesus' return (8:38). But from the moment of his resurrection, Jesus begins to gather his followers into a community of trust and obedience to God and of humble service to others. United to him, this community is now the new temple, filled with God's presence and praise. Exercising his ongoing leadership over this community, Jesus will meet his disciples in Galilee (16:7), that is, in the ordinary circumstances of their lives. He will continue to lead this community in all the Galilees of the world.

Mark, it seems, wrote his Gospel with a twofold pastoral purpose, intending to lead us to a deeper understanding of both the *now* and the *not-yet* aspects of the kingdom that Jesus has brought. He wished us to be confident that the risen Jesus is now leading us on a mission for that kingdom. And he wished us to accept the cross as the starting point for that mission, which looks toward a kingdom not yet fully arrived.

While the absence of a description of the risen Jesus may at first strike us as a shortcoming in Mark's conclusion, in its own way it carries a distinct message. A picture of the risen Jesus might tend to displace in our minds the picture that Mark has already given us. With his empty-tomb ending, Mark leaves us thinking of Jesus with his disciples as they visited the villages of Galilee, walked the roads, and spent their final days in Jerusalem. Mark has given us these scenes of Jesus with his followers in the various settings of their ordinary lives in order to convey his final message: the risen Jesus is with us in the ordinary settings of *our* lives.

Unfinished Business

Jesus and His Followers at the End of Mark's Gospel

The ending that Mark himself gave to his Gospel leaves the story of Jesus' relationship with his disciples unresolved. When Jesus is arrested, his male disciples run away (14:50). The last we see of any of them in Mark's Gospel is Peter, weeping after denying that he knows Jesus (14:72). At least a few of the women disciples remain with Jesus as he dies, watching from a distance (15:40–41). But at the very end the women run away too and do not deliver the report that the angel charges them with (16:8). Mark's ending is, in fact, quite abrupt. The Greek wording of 16:8 literally says that "they told nothing to anyone, they were frightened for." This is only slightly less startling in Greek than in English.

This sudden ending, which leaves important threads dangling, spurs us to ask, "Then what?"

Like us, Mark's original readers probably already knew part of the answer. Eventually the women must have gotten over their fright and told the male disciples what had happened at the tomb, for how else could the incident have become known? Then too, the angel spoke about a meeting between the risen Jesus and his followers that would take place in Galilee (16:7). Mark's readers, being Christians, would have heard about such appearances of Jesus after his resurrection. It is even possible that Mark's original readers heard about these appearances from Peter himself. If the tradition that Mark wrote at Rome is correct, Mark's first readers would have been Roman Christians, who might have had a chance to hear Peter's testimony when he was in Rome before his martyrdom there.

Still, Mark leaves us guessing about what happened when Jesus met his followers in Galilee.

In *The Christology of Mark's Gospel,* biblical scholar Jack D. Kingsbury argues that we can be reasonably sure that at least three things took place. First, he observes, the angel's words in 16:7 ("Go, tell his disciples and Peter that he is going ahead of you to Galilee; there you will see him, just as he told you") call to mind Jesus' promise that they would see him after his resurrection (14:28). Kingsbury points out that Jesus made this promise just after predicting that his disciples would fall away from him and deny him (14:27). "Against this background of failure," Kingsbury writes, "Jesus' promise to the disciples that after his resurrection they will see him . . . means little unless it means first of all that at this meeting he effects a reversal of their failed condition and reconstitutes them as his followers. Accordingly, one thing the reader can project as taking place at this meeting in Galilee is that Jesus reconciles the disciples to himself."

Kingsbury adds, "The second thing the reader can project as taking place is that, in seeing the risen Jesus, the disciples at last penetrate the secret of his identity." They had recognized Jesus as Messiah but had not expected a suffering messiah. They had not known Jesus as the Son of God who would show his utter trust in and obedience to his Father by laying down his life. Seeing the crucified-but-risen one in Galilee, they would be able for the first time to grasp who he really is. As Kingsbury puts it, they would "finally be able to appropriate God's 'evaluative point of view' concerning his identity (9:7) and to 'think' about him aright, that is, as God 'thinks' about him."

In Kingsbury's view, "The third thing the reader can project about the meeting in Galilee is that the disciples, in seeing the risen Jesus, also gain insight into themselves. In perceiving Jesus aright, the disciples likewise perceive themselves aright, which is to say that they grasp the meaning of true discipleship."

In Galilee, we may suppose, the risen Jesus gave his disciples a new chance. He forgave them, healed their spiritual sight, and restored their relationship with him.

There is a circularity to the Gospel of Mark. What occurs at the beginning occurs again after the end. Jesus' first act, after announcing that the kingdom was near, was to call disciples (1:16–20). His first act after rising from the dead will be to gather his disciples around him again. The Gospel begins with John's call to repentance, soon followed by Jesus' acts of forgiveness. The Gospel ends with Jesus' followers, who need to repent, receiving the promise of a meeting with Jesus (16:7) at which they can be reconciled with him.

Perhaps Mark constructed his Gospel in this somewhat circular way because he thought there is also a circularity to the Christian life. His first readers already knew that Jesus is the Messiah and Son of God. They were already committed to following him. But it is possible to make an initial commitment to follow Jesus without understanding thoroughly what that means—or recognizing how unprepared one is to do it. Following Jesus involves a process of discovering that he is somewhat different from what we expect, a process of stumbling along the way, receiving his help and forgiveness, and coming to a deeper knowledge of him. Mark wrote to help his readers reflect on this process. His Gospel was a tool for examining their successes and failures in following Jesus and coming to deeper conversion.

As Mark shows, Jesus' first disciples did not "get it" the first time around. Presumably they did not get it all the second time either. Nor did Mark's first readers, who lived a generation or so later. Nor do we, twenty centuries later.

Like Jesus' first disciples and Mark's first readers, we experience Jesus' call. We set out to follow Jesus, but we inevitably run into difficulties. The kingdom that he leads us into, while filled with God's power, is hidden. God's power sometimes removes evil, but it often manifests itself by enabling us to respond to evil with love, patience, courage, and forgiveness. The kingdom continues to come, as it did through Jesus, through suffering and death. Grasping this kingdom requires faith. It requires seeing things as God sees them, not as we are inclined to see them. Cooperating with Jesus in the coming of this kingdom involves denying ourselves and living for a fulfillment that is yet to come. It involves obedience to God, trust in God, humble service to other people, and participation in a community of fellow followers, the Church.

Talking about all this may be easy. But, like ballet, as soon as we give it a try, we find out how difficult it is. Our blindness to God's ways of working is exposed. Our tendency to look out for ourselves first, our desire to be in charge, our avoidance of grimy, thankless tasks, our thirst for recognition, our fear of identifying ourselves with an unpopular position, our cowardice—all these ordinary, human tendencies immediately come to the surface. It turns out to be much easier to acknowledge Jesus in church on Sunday morning than to seize the weekday opportunities to trust him and serve other people. In real life, the way the suffering Son of God wishes to work is often not very obvious to us or, if we notice it, not very appealing.

So we fail, as Jesus' first disciples did. Like Peter, we may sometimes feel bitterly disappointed with ourselves. We discover our need for conversion. Having experienced our blindness and hard-heartedness, we turn back to Jesus for forgiveness and healing. We too go through a cycle of repentance and reconciliation with him.

This process is what Jesus is about in our lives, as he was in the lives of his first disciples. He foresees our failures as clearly as he foresaw those of his first followers. He is still as Mark shows him: a patient teacher, always willing to forgive, realistic about his followers' shortcomings and hidden flaws but never harsh.

St. Thérèse of Lisieux writes, "This daring ambition of aspiring to great sanctity has never left me. I do not rely on my own merits, because I haven't any. I put all my confidence in him who is virtue, who is holiness itself. My feeble efforts are all he wants; he can lift me up to his side and, by clothing me with his own boundless merits, make a saint of me."

Mark's message, his good news, is that Jesus died as a ransom to establish a bond between God and us. When we stumble in our efforts to follow him, we become especially conscious that this ransom is just what we need. So we can be glad that Jesus ate the Passover with his followers and gave himself to them wholly—and continues to give himself to us in the Eucharist. We can be glad that Jesus met his disciples in Galilee after their failure and reconciled them to himself—and continues to meet us in the sacrament of reconciliation. After his resurrection, Jesus went ahead of the disciples to Galilee, the ordinary sphere of their lives, to lead them on a mission with him. We can be glad that he meets us today wherever we live and keeps calling us to follow him.

Suggestions for Bible Discussion Groups

L ike a camping trip, a Bible discussion group works best if you agree on what you're undertaking together, why you're doing it, where you hope to get to, and how you intend to get there. Many groups use their first meeting to consider such questions. Here is a checklist of issues, with a few bits of advice from people with experience in Bible discussions. (A planning discussion will go more smoothly if the leaders have thought through the following issues beforehand.)

Agree on your purpose. Are you getting together to gain wisdom and direction for your life? to finally get acquainted with the Bible? to support one another in following Christ? to encourage those who are exploring—or reexploring—the Church? for other reasons?

Agree on attitudes. For example: "We're all beginners here." "We're here to help each other understand and respond to God's Word." "We're not here to offer counseling or direction to each other." "We want to read Scripture prayerfully." What do you wish to emphasize? Make it explicit!

Agree on ground rules. Barbara J. Fleischer, in her useful book *Facilitating for Growth,* recommends that a group clearly state its approach to the following:

+ Preparation. Do we agree to read the material before each meeting?

+ Attendance. What kind of priority will we give to our meetings?

+ Self-revelation. Are we willing to gradually help the others in the group get to know us—our weaknesses as well as our strengths, our needs as well as our gifts?

+ Listening. Will we commit ourselves to listen to each other?

+ Confidentiality. Will we keep everything that is shared with the group in the group?

+ Encouragement and support. Will we give as well as receive?

+ Participation. Will we work to allow everyone time and opportunity to make a contribution?

You could probably take a pen and draw a circle around *listening* and *confidentiality*. Those two points are especially important.

The following items could be added to Fleischer's list:

✦ Relationship with parish. Is our group part of the religious education program? independent but operating with the express approval of the pastor? not a parish-based group at all?

✦ New members. In the course of the six meetings, will new members be allowed?

Agree on housekeeping.

✦ When will we meet?

✦ How often will we meet? Weekly or every other week is best if you can manage it. William Riley remarks, "Meetings once a month are too distant from each other for the threads of the last session not to be lost" (*The Bible Study Group: An Owner's Manual*).

✦ How long will meetings run?

✦ Where will we meet?

✦ Is any setup needed? Christine Dodd writes that "the problem with meeting in a place like a church hall is that it can be very soul-destroying" given the cold, impersonal feel of many church facilities. If you have to meet in a church facility, Dodd recommends doing something to make the area homey (*Making Scripture Work*).

✦ Who will host the meetings? Leaders and hosts are not necessarily identical.

✦ Will we have refreshments? Who will provide them?

✦ What about child care? Most experienced leaders of Bible discussion groups discourage bringing infants or other children to adult Bible discussions.

Agree on leadership. You need someone to facilitate—
to keep the discussion on track, to see that everyone has a
chance to speak, to help the group stay on schedule. Rena Duff,
editor of the newsletter *Sharing God's Word Today,* recommends
having two or three people take turns leading the discussions.

It's okay if the leader is not an expert regarding the Bible.
You have this booklet, and if questions come up that no one can
answer, you can delegate a participant to do a little research between meetings. It's important for the leader to set an example of
listening, to draw out the quieter members (and occasionally restrain the more vocal ones), to move the group on when it gets
stuck, to remind the members of their agreements, and to summarize what the group is accomplishing.

Bible discussion is an opportunity to experience the fulfillment of Jesus' promise "Where two or three are gathered in my
name, I am there among them" (Matthew 18:20). Put your discussion group in Jesus' hands. Pray for the guidance of the Spirit. And
have a great time exploring God's Word together!

Suggestions for Individuals

Y ou can use this booklet just as well for individual study as for group discussion. While discussing the Bible with other people can be a rich experience, there are advantages to individual reading. For example:

✦ You can focus on the points that interest you most.

✦ You can go at your own pace.

✦ You can be completely relaxed and unashamedly honest in your answers to all the questions, since you don't have to share them with anyone else!

My suggestions for using this booklet on your own are these:

✦ Don't skip "Questions to Begin." The questions can help you as an individual reader warm up to the topic of the reading.

✦ Take your time on "Questions for Careful Reading" and "Questions for Application." While a group will probably not have enough time to work on all the questions, you can allow yourself the time to consider all of them if you are using the booklet by yourself.

✦ If you are going through Mark at your own pace, consider reading the entire Gospel, not just the parts excerpted in this booklet. "Between Discussions" pages will give you some guidance in reading the additional portions of Mark. Your total understanding of the Gospel will be greatly increased by reading through Mark from beginning to end.

✦ Since you control the pace, give yourself plenty of opportunities to reflect on the meaning of the Gospel for you. Let your reading be an opportunity for Mark's words to become God's words to you.

Bibles

The following editions of the Bible contain the full set of biblical books recognized by the Catholic Church, along with a great deal of useful explanatory material:

✦ The Catholic Study Bible (Oxford University Press), which uses the text of the New American Bible

✦ The Catholic Bible: Personal Study Edition (Oxford University Press), which also uses the text of the New American Bible

✦ The New Jerusalem Bible, the regular (not the standard or reader's) edition (Doubleday)

Books

✦ Ernest Best, *Following Jesus: Discipleship in the Gospel of Mark,* Journal for the study of the New Testament, Supplement Series 4 (Sheffield, England: JSOt Press, 1981).

✦ John Paul Heil, *The Gospel of Mark as Model for Action: A Reader-Response Commentary* (New York: Paulist Press, 1992).

✦ Jack Dean Kingsbury, *The Christology of Mark's Gospel* (Philadelphia: Fortress Press, 1983).

✦ George T. Montague, S.M., *Mark: Good News for Hard Times* (Steubenville, Ohio: Franciscan University Press, 1992).

✦ Lamar Williamson Jr., *Mark,* Interpretation: A Bible Commentary for Teaching and Preaching (Atlanta: John Knox Press, 1983).

How has Scripture had an impact on your life? Was this booklet helpful to you in your study of the Bible? Please send comments, suggestions, and personal experiences to Kevin Perrotta c/o Trade Editorial Department, Loyola Press, 3441 N. Ashland Ave., Chicago, IL 60657.